BRADBURY'S
BOOK OF
HALLMARKS

GW00640862

ONE OF A PAIR OF GEORGE II
SILVER TABLE CANDLESTICKS
Nicholas Sprimont, London, 1746
60 oz. 8 dwt., height 26.8 cm., 10¹/₂ ins.

BRADBURY'S BOOK OF HALLMARKS

A guide to marks of origin on
English, Scottish and Irish silver,
gold and platinum and on
foreign imported silver and gold plate
1544 to 1998

OLD SHEFFIELD PLATE
MAKERS' MARKS
1743 - 1860

Originally compiled by

FREDERICK BRADBURY, F.S.A.
SHEFFIELD, ENGLAND

Published by
FREDERICK BRADBURY PUBLICATIONS LTD.
©

FIRST EDITION: 1927

REVISED: 1928, 1932, 1936,
1939, 1943, 1947, 1950, 1955, 1959,
1964, 1968, 1971, 1973

NEW EDITION: 1975

REVISED: 1976, 1977, 1978, 1979,
1980, 1982, 1984, 1985, 1987, 1988,
1991, 1993, 1997

ISBN 0 9531741 0 7 (Paperback)

ISBN 0 9531741 1 5 (Hardback)

Printed by
Galliard (Printers) Ltd
Queen Anne's Road, Great Yarmouth, NR31 0LL
England
1997

CONTENTS

PREFACE

The Assay Marks depicted in this small work of reference have been collected for a period of over 70 years. Originally, they were assembled and noted at various times by the author and others who collaborated with him and first published in 1927. Since that date, the book has been regularly revised and corrected in the light of continuing research and brought up to date, both by the author until his death and later by others to whom the responsibility of the work was entrusted. The marks have been submitted for investigation to various well known collectors, also the Masters who, in turn, have held office at the Assay Offices in England, Scotland and Ireland. Other sources have been searched for knowledge in connection with articles bearing provincial Assay Marks met with from time to time.

It contains a short explanation of the Hallmarking Act 1973, undoubtedly the most important piece of British legislation to affect the marking of gold and silver wares for over 100 years for, in addition to the changes in the marks on gold and silver effective from 1st January, 1975, the Act also required platinum wares to be marked for the first time.

Also some information on Convention Hallmarks is included. This Convention, originating in EFTA, is the initial step towards obtaining an international system of hallmarking of articles made from precious metals, guaranteeing for the first time, acceptable and mutually agreed standards of fineness.

As this work is published in the form of a handy reference book only, should the reader require more definite particulars concerning the origin, styles and workmanship of the craftsmen associated with the production of Antique Silver, he will find the following published works, where obtainable, of great assistance to him: *English Goldsmiths and their Marks*, by the late Sir Charles J. Jackson, F.S.A., and *The Illustrated History of English Plate*, by the same author. *The Gold and Silver of Windsor Castle; Old Plate of the Cambridge Colleges; Old Silver,*

European & American, etc., by E. Alfred Jones, M.A., F.S.A., F.R.HIST.S., many volumes by the Rev. J. T. Evans, M.A., F.S.A., on *Church Plate,* and *English & Scottish Silver Spoons* by Com. G. E. P. How, R.N., also *English Church Plate* and *English Domestic Silver* by Charles Oman, *Silver* by Gerald Taylor (Pelican) and the V. and A. Museum Handbooks on Silver. Other authors who have written notable works dealing with the subject of Antique Silver are:—Wilfred J. Cripps, C.B., F.S.A., W. W. Watts, F.S.A., Octavius Morgan and W. Chaffers.

ACKNOWLEDGEMENTS

For assistance accorded in
the tabulation of the marks produced in
this small work
we desire to thank the following
gentlemen for the services they have rendered

Mr. H. S. Fothringham.	Aberfeldy
Mr. A. Westwood	Birmingham
Mr. Hamil Westwood	Birmingham
Mr. S. E. F. Beechey	Birmingham
Mr. B. Ward (Assay Master).	Birmingham
Mr. Llewellyn Davies	Cardiff
Mr. Fred Lowe	Chester
Mr. Ronald Le Bas (Assay Master).	Dublin
Mr. J. Harper	Edinburgh
Mr. G. W. M. Crichton.	Edinburgh
Mr. C. Biggs	Exeter
Mr. E. Walker	Glasgow
Messrs. Christie, Manson & Woods	London
Mr. L. Crichton	London
Mr. J. J. Hodges	London
Com. G. E. P. How, R.N.	London
Mr. E. Alfred Jones	London
Mr. A. J. Koop (V. & A. Museum)	London
Mr. G. R. Hughes.	London
Mr. W. A. Prideaux, *Clerk*, Dr. F. Bennett, *Dep. Warden*, Wor. Company of Goldsmiths	London
Mr. C. W. Oakford.	Philadelphia, U.S.A.
Mr. D. G. Johnson	Sheffield
Mr. E. Senior Atkin	Sheffield
Mr. W. F. Northend, F.S.A..	Sheffield
Mr. W. T. Cocks	Sheffield
Capt. S. W. Turner, M.C., F.R.S.A.	Sheffield
Mr. G. H. Eno	Sheffield
Revd. J. T. Evans	Stow-on-the-Wold
Mr. Colin Hawker.	Sutton Coldfield
Mr. H. G. Baker	Swinton, Yorks.
Mr. Arthur J. Hawkes, F.S.A.	Wigan
Major H. N. Robertson.	Wrotham, Kent

AN INTRODUCTION TO HALLMARKING

An explanation of the Assay Offices' devices used in Great Britain and Ireland

MARKS ON SILVER TO 1974

Those who have formed a comprehensive collection of Old English Silver Plate have an advantage in that their acquisitions can be accurately dated and the source of origin located by the series of Hallmarks shown on each article in their possession.

From the end of the 12th century the craft of the silversmith has been regulated in conformity with Royal Ordinances and Acts of Parliament. Consequently, most articles of silver plate bear marks which enable the year, the place of assay and also the maker's name to be definitely traced. Names registered before the end of the 17th century however cannot be identified from marks owing to the plates having been destroyed at the London Goldsmiths' Hall in the Great Fire of 1666. In England, the craft was regulated by the Guild of Goldsmiths at London and in Ireland, by the Guild at Dublin. In Scotland the craft was theoretically supervised by the Edinburgh Goldsmiths' Incorporation, but in practice its influence outside the capital was limited.

The experience gained by centuries of investigation has resulted in the evolution of a complete system of Hallmarking. The same purpose was served at each office by striking a mark, similar in character though different in detail. These marks constitute:

In England, until early in the 17th century, the usual maker's mark was a symbol. Many goldsmiths used a rebus of their names, and initials became more common as the century advanced. From 1696 to 1720 (the Britannia period) the law required the first two letters of the surname to be used. After 1720, initials once more became the norm.

Rebus marks of
John Buck and Thomas Dove

In Scotland, until the early 18th century, the usual maker's mark was a monogram of his initials. The monogram then began to die out, to be replaced by plain initials. Some goldsmiths with short names used their whole names as a mark, e.g. "Ged" and "Tait".

The makers' marks struck on antique silver of all periods are far too numerous to be dealt with in a small work of this description, but it is notable that there are records of Goldsmiths' names to be found dating back to the early years of the Norman Conquest, whilst in the latter part of the 12th century, a "Guild" or association of Goldsmiths and Silversmiths existed in London. In Scotland, individual goldsmiths may be identified from the reign of David I (1124-53) onwards.

MARK OF ORIGIN

The mark of origin, differing at each assay office, was first introduced in London towards the end of the 14th century; this enables the location of the office of assay to be traced, e.g.

Edinburgh   London

Dublin

In England there have been two standards to which silver was assayed, Sterling, 92.5% and Britannia, 95.8%. The Lion Passant was adopted as the Sterling standard mark in London in 1544. By 1696, the conversion of silver coin into plate had so interfered with trade that an Act was passed raising the standard of wrought plate from Sterling to Britannia and the marks required throughout England were a Lion's head erased and the figure of Britannia.

This continued until 1720 when Sterling was restored and the Lion Passant was reinstated. Britannia remained, and remains, an optional higher standard which is still sometimes used by goldsmiths, mostly for prestige pieces.

In Scotland, the official standard, first ordained by Statute in 1457, was 91.6%, and was vouched for by the Deacon's mark until 1681, and thereafter by the Assay Master's mark. This standard remained in force (except for the period 1489-1555 when the "Standard of Bruges" applied) until 1 June 1720, from which time Sterling became the legally required standard, as in England. Britannia became theoretically available at the same time, but no marks seem to have been provided for its use until 1846.

DATE LETTER

Letters of the alphabet are used as marks to enable the date of manufacture to be determined. Date letters before 1975 are best referred to by both the part-years during which they were current, since half their life-time or more occurred during the calendar year following that of their introduction. This effect is particularly noticable in the case of Edinburgh, where the letter was changed annually in September until 1832, and thereafter not until October. In London the change was made in May;

in Birmingham and Sheffield it happened in July; in Dublin it occurred in June until 1932 since when it changes in January. Starting in 1975, all date letters change on 1st January, and so the assay year and calendar year now coincide. The various cycles of date letters may be identified in the tables which follow by the forms of the letters and the shapes of the shields in which they are contained.

DUTY MARK

The Sovereign's Head shows that duty has been paid on the piece bearing it. It appears on all articles made between 1st December, 1784 and 30th April, 1890, except on those articles not liable to compulsory hallmarking and on watchcases after 1798. During that period a tax, varying from time to time, was levied on all silver assayed in Great Britain. At the Dublin Assay Office the Sovereign's head as Duty Mark was not introduced until 1807, and at Glasgow not until 1819.

KING'S JUBILEE MARK

A mark bearing the heads of King George V and Queen Mary was used to commemorate the 25th Anniversary of his Majesty's Accession and may be found on silver plate assayed in the calendar year 1935, accompanied by the date letters for the assay years 1934-35 and 1935-36.

CORONATION MARK

The head of Queen Elizabeth II was marked on silver plate assayed in the calendar year 1953 to commemorate the Coronation of Her Majesty. As most of the assay offices did not change the date letter until about the middle of the year or later, some plate bearing the letter for 1952 will be found with the Coronation Mark as well as 1953.

QUEEN'S JUBILEE MARK

The head of Queen Elizabeth II was used on silver plate assayed in 1977, to commemorate the 25th Anniversary of Her Majesty's Accession.

LONDON

This small book begins with the London Assay Office marks, whilst those used by other offices follow alphabetically. Examples of every known type of silver plate, both decorative and useful, are to be found assayed in London. The Guild mark depicts the Leopard's Head, which varies in aspect from time to time, and is surmounted with a Crown between the years 1478 and 1820 after which date the crown was deleted. The Guild mark was sometimes omitted altogether c.1790-1820, especially on small articles.

The London Silversmiths have maintained a very high standard of design and workmanship throughout the centuries whilst the more notable craftsmen have shown individuality in the conception and execution of their designs to an extent which has won the world's admiration.

BIRMINGHAM

This Office, established by Act of Parliament in 1772, was opened in 1773. Its distinguishing mark is an Anchor, placed on its side for gold, upright for silver, which is accompanied by a Lion Passant, a date letter, duty mark (Sovereign's Head) and maker's initials. Antique silver made in Birmingham includes all forms of domestic plate from the greatest to the least, with a preponderance of the smaller class of goods, viz: vinaigrettes, snuff boxes, buckles, gun furniture and the like.

   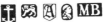

CHESTER

A Guild of Goldsmiths supervised the manufacture, assay and sale of plate in this city as early as the beginning of the 15th century, but the marking was not regulated until towards the close of the 17th century. The marks then used were similar to those found on London Hallmarked silver of the same period, and the sequence of date letters followed in alphabetical order. The distinguishing mark is a shield bearing the Arms of the city. Antique silver plate with the Chester mark thereon is more or less confined to smaller articles in the form of Tankards, Beakers, Tumbler Cups, Pipkins and Cream Jugs. It does not embrace the whole range of the silversmith's craft. The Chester office was closed down on 24th August, 1962.

DUBLIN

The Hallmarking of Irish silver began towards the middle of the 17th century. The mark of origin is the Harp Crowned and it appears with a date letter and maker's mark. In 1731, the figure of Hibernia was added. The whole range of the silversmith's craft is to be found bearing the Dublin assay marks: the workmanship was excellent and the designs were usually of a decorative nature. Dublin absorbed many emigrant goldsmiths after the revocation of the Edict of Nantes in 1685 and their influence can be distinctly traced in the production of Irish silver of the 18th century. The assay office was unaffected by the 1973 British Hallmarking Act.

EDINBURGH

Scottish hallmarks have been regulated by statute since 1457 but the earliest known example dates only from 1556-7. The Incorporation of Goldsmiths of the City of Edinburgh has existed since at least the 1490s and its earliest surviving records date from 1525. The town mark of Edinburgh is a three-towered Castle; this was accompanied by the maker's mark (usually on the left) and the deacon's mark (usually on the right) until 1681, when an assay master was appointed and a date-letter system introduced. We then get the castle, assay master's mark, date letter and maker's mark. In 1759 the assay master's initials were replaced by a Scottish thistle, a practice which continued until 1974. The monarch's head is found as a duty mark from 1784 until 1890. On 1 January 1975 the thistle was replaced by a Lion Rampant. Edinburgh silver exhibits a vigorous and individual Scottishness until the late 18th century when English influences began to be felt.

c.1556   1681

1805    1975

EXETER

Silver plate was made in this ancient city from the very earliest times, and the assay marks date from the middle of the 16th century. The mark of origin was in the form of a letter X usually in a round shield surmounted by a Crown. In 1701 this was replaced by a three towered Castle. Assay marking was conducted somewhat irregularly until the beginning of the 18th century. From 1701-1720, in addition to the town and makers' marks, the Britannia mark and Lion's Head erased, in vogue at other assay offices, were used and these, after 1721, gave place to the Leopard's Head and Lion Passant in square shields.

Much fine plate was made in Exeter, notably, Ecclesiastical Vessels, Tankards, Loving Cups, Caudle Cups and Covers, Coffee Pots and Tea Pots, but very few of the small articles are to be found bearing the Exeter assay marks. There is documentary evidence that late in the 17th century a large number of craftsmen dwelt in the city, but at the end of the 18th century the assaying of silver in Exeter was of a very perfunctory nature, though the right of Hallmarking was exercised intermittently until the year 1882 after which date it ceased entirely.

GLASGOW

Goldsmiths worked in Glasgow from at least as early as the mid-16th century, and maybe earlier, but the first definite marks are not found until the later 17th century. The town mark, based upon the arms of the city, consisted of a Tree, Bird, Bell, Fish and Ring motif, each goldsmith using his own variation up until 1784, with the maker's mark usually struck either side of the town mark. A date-letter cycle was ordered to be introduced in 1681 but was abandoned after twenty-five years or so. During much of the 18th century, random letters, usually S or O, were used as marks, but they were not date letters. Locally struck marks ceased in 1784, from which date virtually all Glasgow work was sent to Edinburgh for assay. Glasgow makers' marks are therefore found with Edinburgh Assay Office marks from 1784 until 1819, when Glasgow got its own assay office, administered by the newly created Glasgow Goldsmiths Company. The Company's marks were: the town mark (already described), a lion rampant (standard mark), a date-letter and the monarch's head (duty mark). A thistle was added to these in 1914.

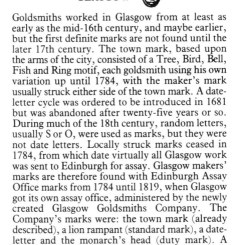

17

NEWCASTLE-ON-TYNE

Silver was assayed here from the middle of the 17th century. The town mark was three separate Castles in a shield but the marking was erratic until 1702, when the figure of Britannia and the Lion's head erased, denoting the new Standard, were first introduced. In 1720, on the restoration of the old standard, the Leopard's Head and Lion Passant were substituted for these two marks and were used with town mark and date letter. The Lion Passant faces to the right from 1721 to 1727.

Much silver was assayed in Newcastle during the early part of the 18th century, chiefly of a domestic kind, such as Coffee Pots and Tea Pots, a particular feature being the large quantity of Tankards and Two-handled Cups produced in this town.

NORWICH

Silver was made in the city from very early times, and assay marks can be traced to the middle of the 16th century, when the mark of origin was a Castle surmounting a Lion Passant used with a date letter and maker's mark.

In the first quarter of the 17th century, a further town mark was added, viz: a Seeded Rose Crowned. During the last half of the century this was altered to a Rose with a stem.

Silver marking was very erratic at this office, and little, if any, silver was assayed after 1701. Some fine examples, made in Norwich, are to be found in the Eastern Counties confined chiefly to church and corporation plate.

SHEFFIELD

This Office, established by Act of Parliament in 1772, was opened in 1773, the first marks being struck on 20th September. Until 1974, the mark of origin on silver was the Crown accompanied by the usual sequence of marks in use at other assay offices. The date letters began in 1773 with the letter E, and were varied irregularly each year until 1824, after which date they were arranged in alphabetical order. A peculiarity of the office was an association in one punch of a date letter and crown between the years 1780 and 1853. All forms of decorative and domestic plate in use during the 18th and 19th centuries are to be found bearing Sheffield Hallmarks. An important feature of the production of Sheffield silversmiths was the making of candlesticks. Numbers of these were purchased by the London and Edinburgh silversmiths who, even subsequent to the establishment of the Sheffield Assay Office, continued to imprint their marks and caused those of their respective offices to be superimposed thereon.

1775
Sheffield Hall Marks

1775
Sheffield marks overstruck at Goldsmiths' Hall, London

1790
Sheffield marks overstruck at Edinburgh Assay Office

YORK

Silver was assayed in this old Yorkshire capital from the middle of the 16th century. The mark of origin was a halved Leopard's Head with a Fleur-de-Lys similarly treated conjoined in one shield. This was used with a sequence of date letters and maker's marks. Towards the end of the 17th century the half Leopard's Head was replaced by a half Seeded Rose. In 1701 the town mark was altered to Five Lions Passant on a Cross. Early pieces of plate made in the city were of fine design

19

and workmanship, closely resembling those of Scandinavian origin, and consist largely of ecclesiastical and domestic plate, notably Caudle Cups and Tankards, both with and without covers. Only a very small number of silver articles was assayed in York between 1700 and 1780, and from 1780 till the close of the office in 1856, those produced were of a very ordinary description and more for domestic use.

SCOTTISH PROVINCIAL MARKS

There were no assay offices in the burghs of Scotland except in Edinburgh and, from 1819 to 1964, in Glasgow. Since the goldsmiths marked their own work for themselves according to their own whims, there is a great diversity of marks within the larger burghs which it is impossible to represent in the confines of this book. Some similar marks come from different places and different marks from the same place. The table on pages 91-2 can only indicate a sample selection.

MINOR GUILDS

Taunton   Cork

Only the more important Minor Guilds of Goldsmiths are tabulated in this book. Much of their work was not officially assayed at all and the marks, which bore a device or initials in repetition to form the marks of origin, were applied by the various makers themselves.

GOLD MARKING TO 1974

From 1300 the standard for gold was $19\frac{1}{3}$ carats and until 1363 the Leopard's Head was the only assay mark struck on gold. In 1363 the maker's mark was introduced and in 1478 the date letter, as for silver, was added. In 1477 the standard was reduced to 18 carat and in 1575 raised to 22 carat. In 1544 the Lion Passant replaced the Leopard's Head as the standard mark. In 1798 the 18 carat standard was reintroduced additional to the 22 carat and the Crown mark used in place of the Lion Passant, the latter, remaining the distinguishing mark for 22 carat until 1844 when the Crown was used for both and the Lion Passant discarded.

In 1854 three lower standards were introduced, 15, 12 and 9, which had no standard mark other than the carat numbers and the carat value in decimals.

In 1932 the 15 and 12 carats were discontinued and a new standard of 14 carat was substituted.

22 carat   18 carat   14 carat   9 carat

Gold standard marks from 1932 onwards

In addition to these distinguishing marks for gold the articles must also be struck with the town mark, date letter and maker's mark.

Between the years 1784 and 1890, the Sovereign's Head was struck to show that duty had been paid. Until 1974, the Sheffield town mark for silver was the crown so for gold it substituted a York Rose which was stamped on all gold wares of whatever carat. In addition, the Crown was punched on 22 and 18 carat gold as at other English assay offices. Sheffield first marked gold on 1st March, 1904.

At Edinburgh, the standard mark used for 22 and 18 carat gold was the Thistle.

Table of principal changes in standard.

Period	Mark		Standard	
1300 to 1476	[crowned mark]	indicating	19⅕	carat
1477 to 1544	,,	,,	18	,,
1544 to 1574	[lion mark]	,,	18	,,
1575 to 1797	,,	,,	22	,,
1798 to 1843	,,	,,	22	,,
and	[crown mark] [18]	,,	18	,,
1844 to 1853	,, 22	,,	22	,,
	,, 18	,,	18	,,
1854 to 1931	,, 22	,,	22	,,
	,, 18	,,	18	,,
	15(·625)	,,	15	,,
	12(·5)	,,	12	,,
	9(·375)	,,	9	,,
1932 to 1974	[crown mark] [22]	,,	22	,,
	,, 18	,,	18	,,
	14(·585)	,,	14	,,
	9(·375)	,,	9	,,

In Dublin the standards are 22, 20 (rarely), 18, 14, 12 and 9 carats. Until 1784 the same marks were used as for silver, the standard being 22 carat. In 1784 the marks for 22 carat became

 date letter maker's mark 22

At the same time a 20 carat standard was introduced with the following additional marks

Also 18 carat with a Unicorn's Head erased and the figure 18

The figures were often stamped by the maker, or, if not, incised by the Assay office. The Crowned Harp was omitted from jewellery and form the lower standards, 15, 12 and 9 carats.

THE HALLMARKING ACT 1973

*A short explanation of the 1973 Hallmarking
Act and its effect on the marking of
silver, gold and platinum with effect from
1st January, 1975.*

Much of the charm and interest in British
hallmarks lies in their variety and individuality.
The autonomy of each Office and the piecemeal
development of the Law over the Centuries
led to many peculiarities in the marks and in
their application. Each Assay Office was
responsible for the design and cutting of its
own punches, thus, for example, the standard
mark for sterling silver (a Lion Passant) was of
quite a different design at each Hall. The
unbroken continuity of marks over the
centuries is unique and of great fascination.

Nevertheless, the prime object of hallmarking is to protect the public against fraud.
If the public cannot readily recognize the
marks and understand their significance, then
for them, hallmarking becomes nothing more
than a lot of esoteric nonsense. Similarly, the
complexity and apparent lack of logic in the
mass of legislation governing hallmarking had
resulted in an urgent need for codification
and simplification.

The Hallmarking Act 1973 tidied up many of the
complexities and anomalies in the Law and
simplified the hallmarks so that they are easier to
understand and recognize, whilst retaining as much
of the interest and tradition as possible.

The existing standards for silver and gold were
retained unchanged, but for the first time platinum
must be hallmarked, at a single standard of 950
parts per thousand.

The general principle behind the new Law,
is that if an article is above a certain weight
(silver 7·8 g, gold 1 g, and platinum 0·5 g*), it
must be hallmarked before it may be described
as silver, gold or platinum as the case may be.

---

*31·1 g = 1 ounce Troy

British hallmarks consist of three marks, in addition to a registered sponsor's mark:

The Standard Mark.

The Assay Office Mark.

The Date Letter.

THE STANDARD MARKS are now identical at all four Assay Offices except in the case of Sterling silver, where the Edinburgh Assay Office will use a Lion Rampant in place of the Lion Passant used by the English Halls.

	Britannia	Sterling
London		
Birmingham		
Sheffield		
Edinburgh		

The Orb surmounted by a Cross is the standard mark for platinum on British wares. At first this was only struck in London and Birmingham, but began in Sheffield on 27th June, 1975 and in Edinburgh on 18th March, 1982.

London
Birmingham
Sheffield
Edinburgh

The Crown now appears on all standards of gold of British origin and the millesimal mark has replaced the carat. It should be emphasized that there is no reduction in standard involved in this change. The standards are still 916·6, 750, 585 and 375 parts per thousand as before. In the same way, Britannia silver is still of the standard 958·4 parts per thousand, although marked 958 on imported wares.

22 carat	916
18 carat	750
14 carat	585
9 carat	375

THE ASSAY OFFICE MARK is unique to each Office.

London uses the Leopard's Head in indentical form on all British wares including Britannia silver: the traditional Lion's Head erased, used on Britannia silver for nearly 300 years, is no more.

Edinburgh continues to use the Castle as before.

Birmingham still uses the Anchor arranged in a different field on silver from that used upon gold and platinum.

Town Mark on   Town Mark on
Silver   Gold and Platinum

The Sheffield Crown used for over two hundred years upon silver has been replaced with the Rose, introduced in 1904 when gold was first assayed there The loss of this widely recognised mark will be much regretted, but it was essential if the marks were to be simplified.

THE DATE LETTER will still be used but it is now common to all four Offices. It will coincide with the calendar year. If a twenty-five year cycle is adopted by the British Hallmarking Council, then the year 2000 will be a date letter 'A'. This would be an aid to memory for antique collectors of the future.

It will be appreciated that the marks described above are only struck on goods of British origin. For imported goods, please see pp. 27 to 34. The illustrations following of the new marks used by each office should be easily understood. One should look carefully for these marks, which will usually, *but not always* appear in the order shown. On articles made up of several parts, the full mark will normally appear on the major piece but subsidiary "part marks" will also appear. Look for these, they are there to protect you.

LONDON	STANDARD MARK	OFFICE MARK	DATE LETTER
Platinum 950			*A*
Gold 22 carat	916		*A*
Silver Britannia			*A*
Sterling			*A*

BIRMINGHAM	STANDARD MARK	OFFICE MARK	DATE LETTER
Platinum 950			*A*
Gold 18 carat	750		*A*

	OFFICE MARK	STANDARD MARK	DATE LETTER
Silver Britannia			*A*
Sterling			*A*

SHEFFIELD	OFFICE MARK	STANDARD MARK	DATE LETTER
Platinum 950			*A*
Gold 14 carat		585	*A*
Silver Britannia			*A*
Sterling			*A*

EDINBURGH	STANDARD MARK	OFFICE MARK	DATE LETTER
Platinum 950			*H*
Gold 9 carat	375		*A*
Silver Britannia			*A*
Sterling			*A*

MARKS ON IMPORTED PLATE

The Customs Act of 1842 made illegal the selling of imported plate either gold or silver in Great Britain and Ireland unless it had been assayed at a British office. In 1867 the Foreign Mark was introduced as an *addition* to the appropriate British Hallmarks.

Foreign Plate made prior to 1800 was exempted by the Customs (Amendment) Act of 1842. The Hallmarking of Foreign Plate Act of 1939 exempted foreign plate which was more than 100 years old. Articles of foreign plate which in the opinion of the Commissioners of Customs may be properly described as hand chased, inlaid, bronzed or filigree work of Oriental pattern were exempted by the Revenue Act of 1884.

In 1904 it was enacted by Order in Council that the carat value of gold should be shown.

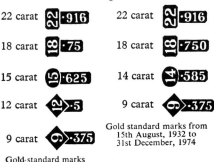

22 carat   •916   22 carat   •916

18 carat   •75   18 carat   •750

15 carat   •625   14 carat   •585

12 carat   •5   9 carat   •375

Gold standard marks from 15th August, 1932 to 31st December, 1974

9 carat   •375

Gold-standard marks from 1904 to 1932

By the same order foreign silver had to be marked with the decimal value of the standard used.

Sterling Standard   •925   Britannia Standard   •9584

In addition the annual date letter and a special assay office mark had to be struck. The F mark was omitted.

Some Town marks were altered by Order in Council in May, 1906, as can be seen by the table below.

The shield containing the Assay Offices Mark for gold is always in a Square with chamfered corners and for silver in a blunt oval.

ASSAY OFFICE MARKS ON IMPORTED PLATE

Assay Office	Period	Gold Mark	Silver Mark
London	1904-06		
	1906-to date		
Birmingham	1904-to date		
Chester	1904-62		
Dublin	1904-06		
	1906-to date		
Edinburgh	1904-to date		
Glasgow	1904-06		
	1906-64		
Sheffield	1904-06		
	1906-to date		

Under the new Hallmarking Act 1973, foreign silver, gold and platinum will in future be marked, as appropriate to the standard, as follows:

Silver	Britannia	**958**
	Sterling	**925**
Gold	22 carat	**916**
	18 carat	**750**
	14 carat	**585**
	9 carat	**375**
Platinum	950	**950**

It will be noted that Britannia silver is now marked 958, not 9584, though there is no diminution in actual standard, and that decimal points are not used.

In addition to the standard marks shown above, a sponsor's mark, together with the town mark and date letter are also struck.

1975 Sheffield Hallmark on Imported 18ct Gold.

The Assay Office Marks on Imported Platinum are as follows:

London	⟨image⟩	Edinburgh	⟨image⟩
Birmingham	⟨image⟩		
Sheffield	⟨image⟩		

HALLMARKING OF PLATINUM

Platinum does not appear in European literature before 1600 when Julius Scalinger* speaks of a white infusible metal found in the mines of Mexico and Darien. As platinum is found in commercial quantities in this district, it is probable that this was the metal to which he referred. It was probably first recognized as a new metal in 1735 by Don Antonio de Alloa in the alluvial deposits in the Rio Pinto in Columbia. Whilst it was worked crudely into ornaments found in South American native graves of ancient date, it was not an easy metal to work and the Spaniards took steps to prevent its export as it was used to adulterate silver and gold.

The metal was experimented with as a curiosity in 18th Century Europe as a result of which, during the 19th Century, it became available in commercial quantities. The development of the Oxy-Hydrogen flame enabled the metal to be worked into jewellery for which purpose it has very desirable properties.

As a precious metal, more costly than gold, which was easily adulterated with less costly metals, it is obvious that a legal standard for the metal and a system of hallmarking was essential to protect the public. In the United Kingdom this has been long overdue since several European countries have controlled the quality of platinum for many years. For example France introduced a system in 1913 and Switzerland a year later. Generally, the standard of 950 parts per thousand was accepted in most countries and the United Kingdom Assay Offices have been urging the adoption of this standard and the introduction of a platinum hallmark for many years. Indeed, the Goldsmiths' Company of London considered introducing private legislation for this purpose in 1924.

---

* "Exercitations Exotericae de Subtilitate".

The Hallmarking Act 1973 sets, for the first time, a legal standard for platinum of 950 parts per thousand and alloys below this standard may not be described as platinum at all. Alloys above this standard which are to be described as platinum must be hallmarked.

In the first instance, as the total demand was likely to be low compared with silver and gold, facilities for platinum assay were set up in London and Birmingham only, Sheffield following on 27th June, 1975.

The 1975 London mark for platinum is:

The method of assay chosen is by means of Atomic absorbtion spectro-photometry, one of the most recent analytical techniques. Gold is assayed by cupellation, the oldest of analytical techniques. Both are the most accurate methods available in their respective fields.

THE BRITISH HALLMARKING COUNCIL

The four United Kingdom Assay Offices were separately constituted as autonomous bodies. For many years they have co-ordinated their activities through a Joint Committee and by consultation between their respective Assay Masters.

The Hallmarking Act 1973 leaves the organization of individual Assay Offices very much as it was, except in so far as it establishes the British Hallmarking Council. This body, established on 1st January, 1974, and becoming operative on 1st January, 1975, is charged with the duty of ensuring that adequate facilities for the assaying of articles of precious metal are available in the United Kingdom, and taking all steps open to them for ensuring the enforcement of the Law. The independent operation of each Assay Office is preserved, but the means for co-ordinating their activities has now been rationalized.

CONVENTION HALLMARKS

The insistence of the United Kingdom upon hallmarking of imported wares has caused problems abroad because ideally goods should be submitted for hallmarking in an unfinished condition. Similarly, there have been problems for United Kingdom manufacturers wishing to export to countries where the United Kingdom hallmark, whilst much sought after, is nevertheless, not legally recognized. The Assay Offices have been very conscious of these problems and have been instrumental in producing through the European Free Trade Association a convention on the control and marking of articles of precious metal. The United Kingdom is a signatory to this convention.

What has been agreed is:

> that the individual national minimum standards of fineness in each contracting state shall be unchanged;

> that approved methods of assay (similar to those in use in the United Kingdom) shall be used in all recognized Assay Offices;

> that a common set of marks be struck.

The United Kingdom ratified the convention in 1976, and other countries which have acceded since, and whose convention marks are recognized in this country are Austria, Denmark, Finland, Ireland, Norway, Portugal, Sweden and Switzerland. Convention hallmarks are struck in addition to, or in place of, the hallmarks of the United Kingdom Assay Offices, although few British manufacturers require this on goods for the home market.

Approved Assay Offices abroad in contracting states, however, strike these marks, which enable the goods bearing them to be sold here without assay in the United Kingdom.

There is provision for occasional checking on these foreign wares and appropriate action will be taken if they are found to be substandard.

Although originating within the European Free Trade Association, there are provisions for any state prepared to meet the basic requirements of the convention to accede.

A convention hallmark will consist of three marks, in addition to a registered sponsor's mark:

A COMMON CONTROL MARK

Gold*	18 carat	
	14 carat	
	9 carat	
Silver*	Sterling†	
Platinum		

A STANDARD OF FINENESS

Gold*	750
	585
	375
Silver*	925†
Platinum	950

AN ASSAY OFFICE MARK
(for Plate made in Britain and Ireland)

	Gold	Silver	Platinum
London			
Birmingham			
Sheffield			
Edinburgh			
Dublin			

*22 carat gold and Britannia silver are not recognised.
†Standards of silver below Sterling (925) not approved in the United Kingdom.

BRITISH AND IRISH ASSAY OFFICE MARKS
(for plate made abroad)

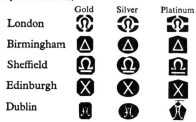

	Gold	Silver	Platinum
London			
Birmingham			
Sheffield			
Edinburgh			
Dublin			

SOME FOREIGN ASSAY OFFICE MARKS
(Certain other domestic marks may also appear).

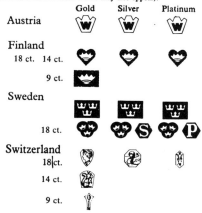

	Gold	Silver	Platinum
Austria			
Finland 18 ct. 14 ct.			
9 ct.			
Sweden			
18 ct.			
Switzerland 18 ct.			
14 ct.			
9 ct.			

(The × denotes a variable sign identifying
the actual Assay Office).

It is unlikely that these marks will acquire the interest to collectors of the traditional United Kingdom marks, if for no other reason than that a date letter will not be struck. Nevertheless the primary purpose of a hallmark guaranteeing the quality of the bullion will be served and the beginnings of international recognition of this fact is an immense step forward.

*Dates of Accession of Sovereigns of England,
showing the main changes in Assay Marks of
the London Office from 1509 and when introduced*

Principal Changes

Henry VIII	. 1509
Edward VI	. 1547
Mary I .	. 1553
Elizabeth I	. 1558
James I .	. 1603
Charles I .	. 1625
Commonwealth	1649
Charles II .	. 1660
James II .	. 1685
William III and Mary II	. 1689
William III	. 1695

1697 Britannia Standard

Anne . . .	1702
George I .	. 1714

1720 Old Standard Restored

George II .	. 1727
George III	. 1760

1784 Duty Mark (Sovereign's head) incuse

1786 Duty Mark in cameo

George IV . 1820

1822 Leopard's Head
uncrowned

William IV . 1830

Victoria . . 1837

1890 Duty Mark ceased

Edward VII . 1901

George V . . 1910

From 1916, sequence on
Sterling Silver is Lion
Passant, Leopard's Head,
Date Letter.

1934-5 Jubilee Mark

Edward VIII . 1936

George VI . 1936

Elizabeth II . 1952

1953 Coronation Mark

1977 Silver Jubilee Mark

Henry VIII 1544	🦁	G	🦁
1545	👑	H	🦁
1546	"	I	"
Edw VI 1547	"	K	"
1548	"	L	🦁
1549	"	M	"
1550	"	N	🦁
1551	👑	O	🦁
1552	"	P	🦁
Mary 1553	"	Q	"
1554	"	R	"
1555	"	S	"
1556	"	T	"
1557	"	V	🦁

LONDON

Elizabeth 1558	𝖆	1578	A	1598	𝕬
1559	𝖇	1579	B	1599	𝕭
1560	𝖈𝖈	1580	C	1600	𝕮
1561	𝖉	1581	D	1601	𝕯
1562	𝖊	1582	E	1602	𝕰
1563	𝖋	1583	F	Jas. 1 1603	𝕱
1564	𝖌	1584	G	1604	𝕲
1565	𝖍	1585	H	1605	𝕳
1566	𝖎	1586	I	1606	𝕴
1567	𝖐𝖐	1587	K	1607	𝕶
1568	𝖑	1588	L	1608	𝕷
1569	𝖒	1589	M	1609	𝕸
1570	𝖓	1590	N	1610	𝕹
1571	𝖔	1591	O	1611	𝕺
1572	𝖕	1592	P	1612	𝕻
1573	𝖖	1593	Q	1613	𝕼
1574	𝖗	1594	R	1614	𝕽
1575	𝖘𝖘	1595	S	1615	𝕾
1576	𝖙	1596	T	1616	𝕿
1577	𝖚	1597	V	1617	𝖁

LONDON

Year	Mark	Year	Mark	Year	Mark
1618	a	1638	a	1658	A
1619	b	1639	B	1659 / Chas. II. 1660	C
1620	c	1640	C	1661	D
1621	d	1641	g	1662	E
1622	e	1642	f	1663	F
1623	f	1643	ff	1664	G
1624 / Chas. I 1625	g / h	1644	Φ	1665	H
1626	i	1645	R	1666	J
1627	k	1646	g	1667	K
1628	l	1647	B	1668	L
1629	m	1648 / Comwth. 1649	C / D	1669	M
1630	n	1650	R	1670	N
1631	o	1651	S	1671	O
1632	p	1652	p	1672	PP
1633	q	1653	q	1673	Q
1634	r	1654	R	1674	R
1635	s	1655	O	1675	S
1636	t	1656	T	1676	T
1637	v	1657	B	1677	U

39

LONDON

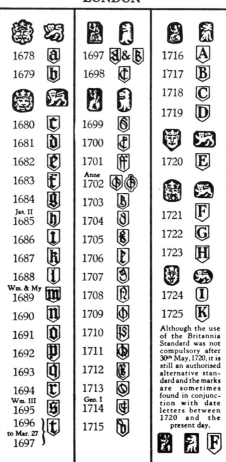

1678	1697	1716 A
1679	1698	1717 B
1680	1699	1718 C
1681	1700	1719 D
1682	1701	1720 E
1683	Anne 1702	1721 F
1684	1703	1722 G
Jas. II 1685	1704	1723 H
1686	1705	1724 I
1687	1706	1725 K
1688	1707	
Wm. & My 1689	1708	
1690	1709	
1691	1710	
1692	1711	
1693	1712	
1694	1713	
Wm. III 1695	Geo. I 1714	
1696 to Mar. 27 1697	1715	

Although the use of the Britannia Standard was not compulsory after 30th May, 1720, it is still an authorised alternative standard and the marks are sometimes found in conjunction with date letters between 1720 and the present day.

40

LONDON

1726 Geo. II.	L	1736	a	1756	A
1727	M	1737	b	1757	B
1728	N	1738	c	1758	C
		1739	d	1759 Geo. III.	D
1729	O	1739	d	1760	E
1730	P	1740	e	1761	F
1731	Q	1741	f	1762	G
1732	R	1742	g	1763	H
1733	S	1743	h	1764	I
1734	T	1744	i	1765	k
1735	V	1745	k	1766	L
		1746	l	1767	M
		1747	m	1768	N
		1748	n	1769	O
This shield is also found occasionally between the years 1716 and 1728.		1749	o	1770	P
		1750	p	1771	Q
				1772	R
		1751	q	1773	S
Numerous variations of the Leopard's Head and Lion passant occur between 1719 and 1729.		1752	r	1774	T C
		1753	ſ	1775	U
		1754	t		
		1755	u		

LONDON

Mark	Letter	Head	Mark	Letter	Head	Mark	Letter	Head
🛡🦁 or 🦁			🛡 🦁 😐			🛡 🦁 😐		
1776	**a**		1796	**A**	,,	1816	**a**	,,
1777	**b**		1797	**B**	,,	1817	**b**	,,
1778	**c**		1798	**C**	,,	1818	**c**	,,
1779	**d**		1799	**D**	,,	1819	**d**	,,
1780	**e**		1800	**E**	,,	Geo. IV. 1820	**e**	,,
1781	**f**		1801	**F**	,,	1821	**f**	,,
1782	**g**		1802	**G**	,,	🦁 🦁 😐		
1783	**h**		1803	**H**	,,	1822	**g**	,,
1784	**i**	👑	1804	**I**	,,	1823	**h**	,,
1785	**k**	,,	1805	**K**	,,	1824	**i**	,,
1786	**l**	👑	1806	**L**	,,	1825	**k**	,,
1787	**m**	,,	1807	**M**	,,	1826	**l**	,,
1788	**n**	,,	1808	**N**	,,	1827	**m**	,,
1789	**o**	,,	1809	**O**	,,	1828	**n**	,,
1790	**p**	,,	1810	**P**	,,	1829	**o**	,,
1791	**q**	,,	1811	**Q**	,,	Wm. IV. 1830	**p**	,,
1792	**r**	,,	1812	**R**	,,	1831	**q**	,,
1793	**s**	,,	1813	**S**	,,	1832	**r**	,,
1794	**t**	,,	1814	**T**	,,	1833	**s**	,,
1795	**u**	,,	1815	**U**	,,	1834	**t**	😐
						1835	**u**	,,

Duty increase shapes also occur in years
1797 ◯ or ◖; 1804 ◠; 1815 ◯ or ◠.

New light on plate duty and its marks
A. B. L. Dove: *ANTIQUE COLLECTING*, Sept. 1984

Leopard's Head crowned and uncrowned in use 1821/2.

LONDON

🛡️	🦁	👑		🛡️	🦁	👑		🛡️	🦁	👑
1836 Vict.	𝕬	,,		1856	𝖆	,,		1876	𝕬𝕬	,,
1837	𝕭	,,		1857	𝖇	,,		1877	𝕭	,,
1838	𝕮	👑		1858	𝖈	,,		1878	𝕮	
1839	𝕯	,,		1859	𝖉	,,		1879	𝕯	,,
1840	𝕰	,,		1860	𝖊	,,		1880	𝕰	,,
1841	𝕱	,,		1861	𝖋	,,		1881	𝕱	,,
1842	𝕲	,,		1862	𝖌	,,		1882	𝕲	,,
1843	𝕳	,,		1863	𝖍	,,		1883	𝕳	,,
1844	𝕵	,,		1864	𝖎	,,		1884	𝕴	,,
1845	𝕶	,,		1865	𝖐	,,		1885	𝕶	,,
1846	𝕷	,,		1866	𝖑	,,		1886	𝕷	,,
1847	𝕸	,,		1867	𝖒	,,		1887	𝕸	,,
1848	𝕹	,,		1868	𝖓	,,		1888	𝕹	,,
1849	𝕺	,,		1869	𝖔	,,		1889	𝕺	,,
1850	𝕻	,,		1870	𝖕	,,		1890	𝕻	,,
1851	𝕼	,,		1871	𝖖	,,		1891	𝕼	
1852	𝕽	,,		1872	𝖗	,,		1892	𝕽	
1853	𝕾	,,		1873	𝖘	,,		1893	𝕾	
1854	𝕿	,,		1874	𝖙	,,		1894	𝕿	
1855	𝖀	,,		1875	𝖚	,,		1895	𝖀	

This shield, without point, is also found between the years 1776 and 1875, usually on small articles.

Queen's Head not used after 1890

43

LONDON

1896 **a**	1916 **a**	Edw. VIII 1936 **A**
1897 **b**	1917 **b**	Geo. VI 1937 **B**
1898 **c**	1918 **c**	1938 **C**
1899 **d**	1919 **d**	1939 **D**
1900 **e**	1920 **e**	1940 **E**
Edw. VII 1901 **f**	1921 **f**	1941 **F**
1902 **g**	1922 **g**	1942 **G**
1903 **h**	1923 **h**	1943 **H**
1904 **i**	1924 **i**	1944 **I**
1905 **k**	1925 **k**	1945 **K**
1906 **l**	1926 **l**	1946 **L**
1907 **m**	1927 **m**	1947 **M**
1908 **n**	1928 **n**	1948 **N**
1909 **o**	1929 **o**	1949 **O**
Geo. V. 1910 **p**	1930 **p**	1950 **P**
1911 **q**	1931 **q**	1951 **Q**
1912 **r**	1932 **r**	Eliz. II 1952 **R**
1913 **s**	1933 **s**	1953 **S**
1914 **t**	1934 **t**	1954 **T**
1915 **u**	1935 **u**	1955 **U**

Britannia Standard
Marks for 1927.

m

44

LONDON

1956	a	1975	A	1991	R
1957	b	1976	B	1992	S
1958	c			1993	T
1959	d	1977	C	1994	U
1960	e			1995	V
1961	f	1978	D	1996	W
1962	g	1979	E	1997	X
1963	h	1980	F	1998	Y
1964	i	1981	G		
1965	k	1982	H		
1966	l	1983	I		
1967	m	1984	K		
1968	n	1985	L		
1969	o	1986	M		
1970	p	1987	N		
1971	q	1988	O		
1972	r	1989	P		
1973	s	1990	Q		
1974	t				

Sequence discontinued upon introduction of new marks under Hallmarking Act 1973.

BIRMINGHAM

1773	A	A A
1774	B	
1775	C	
1776	D	
1777	E	
1778	F	
1779	G	
1780	H	
1781	I	
1782	K	
1783	L	
1784	M	(head)
1785	N	,,
1786	O	(head)
1787	P	,,
1788	Q	,,
1789	R	,,
1790	S	,,
1791	T	,,
1792	U	,,
1793	V	,,
1794	W	,,
1795	X	,,
1796	Y	,,
1797	Z	,,

1798	a	,,
1799	b	,,
1800	c	,,
1801	d	,,
1802	e	,,
1803	f	,,
1804	g	,,
1805	h	,,
1806	i	,,
1807	j	,,
1808	k	,,
1809	l	(head)
1810	m	,,
1811	n	,,
1812	o	,,
1813	p	,,
1814	q	,,
1815	r	,,
1816	s	,,
1817	t	,,
1818	u	,,
1819	v	,,
Geo. IV. 1820	w	,,
1821	x	,,
1822	y	,,
1823	z	,,

1824	A	,,
1825	B	,,
1826	C	,,
1827	D	,,
1828	E	,,
Wm. IV. 1829	F	,,
1830	G	,,
1831	H	(head)
1832	J	,,
1833	K	,,
1834	L	(head)
1835	M	,,
1836	N	,,
Vict. 1837	O	,,
1838	P	(head)
1839	Q	,,
1840	R	,,
1841	S	,,
1842	T	,,
1843	U	,,
1844	U	,,
1845	W	,,
1846	X	,,
1847	Y	,,
1848	Z	,,

In 1797 the duty on silver was doubled, and for a short
time the King's Head was duplicated

BIRMINGHAM

1849	A	,,	1867	S	,,	1883	i	,,
1850	B	,,	1868	T	,,	1884	k	,,
1851	C	,,	1869	U	,,	1885	l	,,
1852	D	,,	1870	V	,,	1886	m	,,
1853	E	,,	1871	W	,,	1887	n	,,
1854	F	,,	1872	X	,,	1888	o	,,
1855	G	,,	1873	Y	,,	1889	p	,,
1856	H	,,	1874	Z	,,	1890	q	,,
1857	I	,,				1891	r	
1858	J	,,	1875	a	,,	1892	s	
1859	K	,,	1876	b	,,	1893	t	
1860	L	,,	1877	c	,,	1894	u	
1861	M	,,	1878	d	,,	1895	v	
1862	N	,,	1879	e	,,	1896	w	
1863	O	,,	1880	f	,,	1897	x	
1864	P	,,	1881	g	,,	1898	y	
1865	Q	,,	1882	h	,,	1899	Z	
1866	R	,,						

BIRMINGHAM

Year	Mark	Year	Mark	Year	Mark
1900	a	1918	t	1934	K
Edw. VII 1901	b	1919	u	1935	L
1902	c	1920	v	Edw. VIII 1936	M
1903	d	1921	w	Geo. VI 1937	N
1904	e	1922	x	1938	O
1905	f	1923	y	1939	P
1906	g	1924	z	1940	Q
1907	h			1941	R
1908	i	1925	A	1942	S
1909	k	1926	B	1943	T
Geo. V 1910	l	1927	C	1944	U
1911	m	1928	D	1945	V
1912	n	1929	E	1946	W
1913	o	1930	F	1947	X
1914	p	1931	G	1948	Y
1915	q	1932	H	1949	Z
1916	r	1933	J		
1917	s				

BIRMINGHAM

1950	A	1966	R	1978	D
1951	B	1967	S	1979	E
Eliz. II 1952	C	1968	T	1980	F
1953	D	1969	U	1981	G
1954	E	1970	V	1982	H
1955	F	1971	W	1983	I
1956	G	1972	X	1984	K
1957	H	1973	Y	1985	L
1958	I			1986	M
1959	K			1987	N
1960	L			1988	O
1961	M	1974	Z	1989	P
1962	N			1990	Q
1963	O	1975	A	1991	R
1964	P	1976	B	1992	S
1965	Q			1993	T
		1977	C	1994	U
				1995	V
				1996	W

Special mark used in 1973 to commemorate bi-centenary of Birmingham Office.

1997		
1998		

CHESTER

1680			1701 Anne	A	1726 Geo. II	A
			1702	B	1727	B
1690			1703	C	1728	C
			1704	D	1729	D
1690 to 1700 STERLING			1705	E	1730	E
			1706	F	1731	F
			1707	G	1732	G
			1708	H	1733	H
			1709	I	1734	J
			1710	K	1735	K
			1711	L	1736	L
			1712	M	1737	M
			1713 Geo. I 1714	N	1738	N
			1715	O	1739	O
			1716	P	1740	P
			1717	Q	1741	Q
			1718	R	1742	R
				S	1743	S
			1719	T	1744	T
			1720	U	1745	U
			1721	V	1746	V
			1722	W	1747	W
			1723	X	1748	X
			1724	Y	1749	Y or Y
			1725	Z	1750	Z

51

CHESTER

1751	ⓐ		1776	ⓐ		1797	Ⓐ	"		
1752	ⓑ		1777	ⓑ		1798	Ⓑ	"		
1753	ⓒ		1778	ⓒ		1799	Ⓒ	"		
1754	ⓓ									
1755	ⓔ		1779	ⓓ		1800	Ⓓ	"		
1756	ⓕ		1780	ⓔ		1801	Ⓔ	"		
1757	Ⓖ		1781	ⓕ		1802	Ⓕ	"		
1758	Ⓗ		1782	ⓖ		1803	Ⓖ	"		
1759 Geo. III	ⓘ		1783	ⓗ		1804	Ⓗ	"		
1760	ⓚ					1805	Ⓘ	"		
1761	ⓛ		1784	ⓘ	"					
1762	ⓜ		1785	ⓚ	"	1806	Ⓚ	"		
1763	ⓝ		1786	ⓛ		1807	Ⓛ	"		
1764	ⓞ		1787	ⓜ	"	1808	Ⓜ	"		
1765	Ⓟ		1788	ⓝ	"	1809	Ⓝ	"		
1766	Ⓠ		1789	ⓞ	"	1810	Ⓞ	"		
1767	Ⓡ		1790	ⓟ	"	1811	Ⓟ	"		
1768	Ⓢ		1791	ⓠ	"	1812	Ⓠ	"		
1769	Ⓣ		1792	ⓡ	"	1813	Ⓡ	"		
1770	Ⓣ		1793	Ⓢ	"	1814	Ⓢ	"		
1771	Ⓤ		1794	ⓣ	"	1815	Ⓣ	"		
1772	Ⓥ		1795	ⓤ	"	1816	Ⓤ	"		
1773	Ⓦ		1796	Ⓥ	"	1817	Ⓥ	"		
1774	Ⓧ									
1775	Ⓨ									

CHESTER

Year		Year		Year	
1818	A	1839	A	1864	a
1819	B	1840	B	1865	b
Geo. IV 1820	C	1841	C	1866	c
1821	D	1842	D	1867	d
1822	D	1843	E	1868	e
		1844	F	1869	f
		1845	G	1870	g
1823	E	1846	H	1871	h
1824	F	1847	J	1872	i
1825	G	1848	K	1873	k
1826	H	1849	L	1874	l
1827	I	1850	M	1875	m
1828	K	1851	N	1876	n
1829	L	1852	O	1877	o
Wm. IV 1830	M	1853	P	1878	p
1831	N	1854	Q	1879	q
1832	O	1855	R	1880	r
1833	P	1856	S	1881	s
1834	Q	1857	T	1882	t
1835	R	1858	U	1883	u
1836	S	1859	V		
Vict. 1837	T	1860	W		
1838	U	1861	X		
		1862	Y		
		1863	Z		

CHESTER

1884	A
1885	B
1886	C
1887	D
1888	E
1889	F
1890	G
1891	H
1892	I
1893	K
1894	L
1895	M
1896	N
1897	O
1898	P
1899	Q
1900	R

Since 1839 both shields have been in use for the Sterling Mark and since 1900 for the Date Letter also.

Edw. VII	
1901	A
1902	B
1903	C
1904	D
1905	E
1906	F
1907	G
1908	H
1909	I
Geo. V	
1910	K
1911	L
1912	M
1913	N
1914	O
1915	P
1916	Q
1917	R
1918	S
1919	T
1920	U
1921	V
1922	W
1923	X
1924	Y
1925	Z

1926	a
1927	b
1928	c
1929	d
1930	e
1931	ff
1932	g
1933	h
1934	i
1935	k
Edw. VIII	
1936	l
Geo. VI	
1937	m
1938	n
1939	o
1940	p
1941	q
1942	r
1943	s
1944	t
1945	u
1946	v
1947	w

54

🦁 🛡	
1948 🅇	
1949 🅨	
1950 🅩	

1951 🄰	
🦁 🛡 🌐 Eliz. II	
1952 🄱	
1953 🄲	
🦁 🛡	
1954 🄳	
1955 🄴	
1956 🄵	
1957 🄶	
1958 🄷	
1959 🄹	
1960 🄺	
1961 🄻	
1st July to 24 Aug. 1962 🄼	

The Chester
Assay Office
closed 24th
August, 1962

Chas. I 1638	A
1639	B
1640	C
1641	D
1642	E
1643	F
1644	G
1645	H
1646	I
1647	K
1648	L
Com'w'th 1649	M
1650	N
1651	O
1652	P
1653	Q
1654	R
1655	S
1656	T
1657	U

1658	a
1659	b
Chas. II 1660	c
1661	d
1662	e
1663	f
1664	g
1665	h
1666	i
1667	k
1668	l
1669	m
1670	n
1671	o
1672	p
1673	q
1674	r
1675	s
1676	t
1677	u

1678	A
1679	B
1680	C
1681	D
1682	E
1683-4	F
Jas. II 1685-7	G
1688-93	h
Wm. III 1694-5	k
1696-8	L
1699	M
1700	N
1701	O
Anne 1702	P
1703	Q
1704-5	R
1706-7	S
1708-9	T
1710-11	U
1712-13	W
Geo. I 1714	X
1715	Y
1716	Z

56

DUBLIN

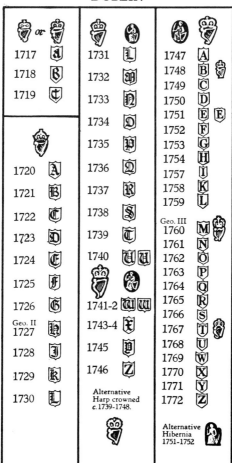

1717	1731	1747 A
1718	1732	1748 B
1719	1733	1749
	1734	1750 D
1720 A	1735	1751 E
1721 B	1736	1752 F
1722 C	1737	1753 G
1723 D	1738	1754 H
1724 E	1739	1757 I
1725 F	1740	1758 K
1726 G		1759 L
Geo. II 1727 H	1741-2	Geo. III 1760 M
1728 I	1743-4	1761
1729 k	1745	1762 N
1730 L	1746 Z	1763 O

Geo. II 1727

Alternative
Harp crowned
c.1739-1748.

Alternative
Hibernia
1751-1752

57

DUBLIN

Year	Letter		Year	Letter	
1773	A		1797	A	
1774	B		1798	B	
1775	C		1799	C	
1776	D		1800	D	
1777	E		1801	E	
1778	F		1802	F	
1779	G		1803	G	
1780	H		1804	H	
1781	I		1805	I	
1782	K		1806	K	
1783	L		1807	L	
1784	M		1808	M	"
1785	N		1809	N	
1786	O				
1787	P		1810	O	"
1788	Q		1811	P	"
1789	R		1812	Q	"
1790	S		1813	R	"
1791	T		1814	S	"
1792	U		1815	T	"
			1816	U	"
1793	W		1817	W	"
1794	X		1818	X	"
1795	Y		1819	Y	"
1796	Z		1820 Geo. IV	Z	"

58

DUBLIN

Throughout this cycle the shape of the shield varies considerably

Year					Year				
1821		A			1837 Vict.		R		
1822	,,	B	,,		1838	,,	S	,,	
1823	,,	C	,,	,,	1839		T		,,
1824	,,	D	,,	,,	1840	,,	U	,,	,,
1825	,,	E e	,,	,,	1841	,,	V	,,	,,
1826	,,	F	,,	,,	1842		W		,,
1827		G			1843	,,	X	,,	,,
1828		H			1844		Y		,,
1829		I			1845		Z		
1830 Wm.IV		K			1846		a		
1831		L			1847	,,	b	,,	,,
1832	,,	M	,,	,,	1848	,,	c	,,	,,
1833		N			1849	,,	d	,,	,,
1834		O			1850	,,	e	,,	,,
1835	,,	P	,,	,,	1851		f f	,,	,,
1836	,,	Q	,,	,,	1852	,,	g g	,,	,,
					1853	,,	h h	,,	,,
					1854	,,	j	,,	,,

59

DUBLIN

1855	k	,,	1871	A	,,
1856	l	,,	1872	B	,,
			1873	C	,,
1857	m	,,	1874	D	,,
1858	n	,,	1875	E	,,
			1876	F	,,
1859	O	,,	1877	G	,,
1860	P	,,	1878	H	,,
			1879	I	,,
1861	Q	,,	1880	K	,,
1862	r	,,	1881	L	,,
			1882	M	,,
1863	S	,,	1883	N	,,
			1884	O	,,
1864	t	,,	1885	P	,,
			1886	Q	,,
1865	u	,,	1887	R	,,
1866	V	,,	1888	S	,,
			1889	T	,,
1867	W	,,	1890	U	,,
			1891	V	,,
1868	X	,,	1892	W	,,
1869	Y	,,	1893	X	,,
			1894	Y	,,
1870	Z	,,	1895	Z	,,

DUBLIN

Year	Letter	Year	Letter	Year	Letter
1896	A	1916	A	Geo. VI 1937	V
1897	B	1917	b	1938	W
1898	C	1918	C	1939	X
1899	D	1919	D	1940	Y
1900	E	1920	e	1941	Z
Edw. VII 1901	F	1921	F		
1902	G	1922	g	1942	A
1903	H	1923	h	1943	B
1904	H	1924	i	1944	C
1905	K	1925	k	1945	D
1906	L	1926	l	1946	E
1907	M	1927	m	1947	F
1908	N	1928	n	1948	G
1909 Geo. V 1910	P	1929	o	1949	H
1911	Q	1930-31	P	1950	I
1912	R	1932	Q	1951	J
1913	S	1933	R	Eliz. II 1952	K
1914	T	1934	S	1953	L
1915	U	1935	T	1954	M
		Edw. VIII 1936	U		

Up to 1931 the date letter was changed on 1st June. The Q of 1932 began on 1st January.

61

DUBLIN

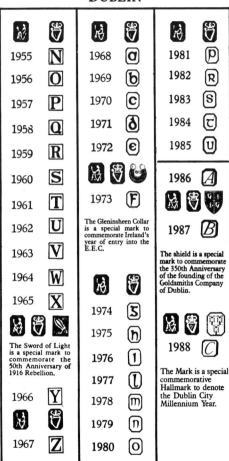

1955	N
1956	O
1957	P
1958	Q
1959	R
1960	S
1961	T
1962	U
1963	V
1964	W
1965	X

The Sword of Light is a special mark to commemorate the 50th Anniversary of 1916 Rebellion.

| 1966 | Y |
| 1967 | Z |

1968	a
1969	b
1970	c
1971	d
1972	e
1973	f

The Gleninsheen Collar is a special mark to commemorate Ireland's year of entry into the E.E.C.

1974	s
1975	h
1976	i
1977	l
1978	m
1979	n
1980	o

1981	p
1982	R
1983	S
1984	T
1985	U

| 1986 | A |
| 1987 | B |

The shield is a special mark to commemorate the 350th Anniversary of the founding of the Goldsmiths Company of Dublin.

| 1988 | C |

The Mark is a special commemorative Hallmark to denote the Dublin City Millennium Year.

DUBLIN

1989 *D*		
1990 *E*		
1991 *F*		
1992 *G*		
1993 *H*		
1994 *I*		
1995 *J*		
1996 *K*		
1997 *L*		
1998 *M*		

EDINBURGH

	TOWN MARK	DEACON'S MARK		TOWN MARK	DEACON'S MARK		TOWN MARK	ASSAY MASTER'S MARK
c.1556	🏰	E	c.1616-35				🏰	B
c.1563	"	IC		🏰	G	1681		a
c.1565	"	🏰	c.1637	🏰	IS		🏰	B
c.1575	🏰	🏰	c.1640	🏰	CT	1682		b
c.1576	🏰	⚓	c.1642	"	IF	1683		c
c.1577	"	🅦	c.1643	🏰	"	1684		d
c.1585	"	M	c.1644	"	A	1685		e
1591	"	🏰	c.1649	"	GC	1686		f
c.1598	🏰	EH	c.1651	"	IF	1687		g
c.1609	"	R	1660	"	KB	1688 Wm. & Mary 1689		h
c.1611	🏰	D	c.1663-81	"	E	1690		i
1613-21			c.1665	"	IS	1691		k
	🏰	S	c.1669	"	R	1692		l
c.1617	🏰	II	c.1675	"	W	1693		m
c.1617	"	G				1694 Wm.III 1695		n
						1696		o
								p
							🏰	P
						1697		r

NOTE: The above dates are greatly simplified, as some deacons held office many times.

64

EDINBURGH

🏰	🅿	🏰	**EP**	🏰	**AU**
1698	𝕾	Geo. I. 1714	**K**	1730	**A**
1699	𝕿	1715	**L**	1731	**B**
1700	𝖚	1716	**M**	1732	**C**
1701	𝖜	1717	**N**	1733	**D**
Anne 1702	🏰 𝖄	🏰	**EP**	1734	**E**
1703	𝖅	1718	**O**	1735	**F**
1704	𝖟	1719	**P P**	1736	**G**
🏰	🅿	🏰	**EP**	1737	**H**
1705	**A**	1720	**Q**	1738	**I**
1706	**B**	1721	**R**	1739	**K**
🏰	**EP**	1722	**S**	🏰	**GED**
1707	**C**	1723	**T**	1740	**L**
1708	**D**	1724	**U**	1741	**M**
1709	**E**	1725	**V V**	🏰	**EL**
1710	**F**	1726 Geo. II.	**W**	1742	**N**
1711	**G**	1727	**X**	1743	**O**
🏰	**EP**	1728	**Y**	🏰	**HG**
1712	**H**	1729	**Z**	1744	**P**
1713	**I**			1745	**Q**
				1746	**R**

65

EDINBURGH

1747	S	1763	J	1780	A	
1748	T	1764	k	1781	B	
1749	U	1765	L	1782	C	
1750	V	1766	M	1783	D	
1751	W	1767	N	1784	E	
1752	X	1768	O	1785	F	"
1753	Y	1769	P	1786	G	
1754	Z	1770	Q	1787	"	"
		1771 ★	R	1788	H	"
1755	A	1772	S	1789	I J	"
1756	B	1773	T	1790	K	"
1757	C	1774	U	1791	L	"
1758	D	1775	V	1792 †	M	. "
1759	E	1776	X	1793	N N	"
Geo. III. 1760	F	1777	Y	1794	O O	"
1761	G	1778	Z	1795	P	"
1762	H	1779	U	1796	Q	"

★ Alternative Town Marks about 1771

† Alternative Town Marks for 1792

66

Year	Mark		Year	Mark		Year	Mark	
1797	R R	🛡	1813	h	🛡	1832	A	🛡
1798	S	,,	1814	i	,,	1833	B	,,
			1815	j	,,	1834	C	,,
1799	T	🛡	1816	k	,,	1835	D	,,
1800	U	,,	1817	l	,,	1836	E	,,
1801	V	,,	1818	m	,,	Vict. 1837	f	,,
			1819	n	,,	1838	G	,,
1802	W	🛡				1839	H	,,
1803	X	,,	Geo. IV 1820	O	🛡	1840	J	,,
1804	Y	,,	1821	P	,,	1841	K	🛡
1805	Z	,,	1822	q	,,	1842	L	,,
			1823	r	,,	1843	M	,,
1806	a	🛡				1844	N	,,
1807	b	,,	1824	S	🛡	1845	O	,,
1808	C	,,	1825	t	,,	1846	P	,,
			1826	U	🛡	1847	Q	,,
1809	d	🛡	1827	V	,,	1848	R	,,
1810	e	,,	1828	W	,,	1849	S	,,
1811	f	,,	1829	X	,,	1850	T	,,
1812	g	,,	Wm. IV 1830	y	,,	1851	U	,,
			1831	Z	,,	1852	V	,,
						1853	W	,,
						1854	X	,,
						1855	Y	,,
						1856	Z	,,

EDINBURGH

1857	Ⓐ	1875	Ⓣ	1890	ⓘ
1858	Ⓑ	1876	Ⓤ	1891	ⓚ
1859	Ⓒ	1877	Ⓥ	1892	ⓛ
1860	Ⓓ	1878	Ⓦ	1893	ⓜ
1861	Ⓔ	1879	Ⓧ	1894	ⓝ
1862	Ⓕ	1880	Ⓨ	1895	ⓞ
1863	Ⓖ	1881	Ⓩ	1896	ⓟ
1864	Ⓗ			1897	ⓠ
1865	Ⓘ			1898	ⓡ
1866	Ⓚ	1882	ⓐ	1899	ⓢ
1867	Ⓛ	1883	ⓑ	1900	ⓣ
1868	Ⓜ	1884	ⓒ	Edw.VII 1901	ⓥ
1869	Ⓝ	1885	ⓓ	1902	ⓦ
1870	Ⓞ	1886	ⓔ	1903	ⓧ
1871	Ⓟ	1887	ⓕ	1904	ⓨ
1872	Ⓠ	1888	ⓖ	1905	ⓩ
1873	Ⓡ	1889	ⓗ		
1874	Ⓢ				

EDINBURGH

1906	Ⓐ	1924	Ⓣ	1939	𝒥		
1907	Ⓑ	1925	Ⓤ	1940	𝒦		
1908	Ⓒ	1926	Ⓥ	1941	𝓛		
1909	Ⓓ	1927	Ⓦ	1942	𝓜		
Geo. V 1910	Ⓔ	1928	Ⓧ	1943	𝒩		
1911	Ⓕ	1929	Ⓨ	1944	𝒪		
1912	Ⓖ	1930	Ⓩ	1945	𝒫		
1913	Ⓗ			1946	𝒬		
1914	Ⓘ	1931	𝒜	1947	𝓡		
1915	Ⓚ	1932	𝓑	1948	𝒮		
1916	Ⓛ	1933	𝒞	1949	𝒯		
1917	Ⓜ	1934	𝒟	1950	𝒰		
1918	Ⓝ	1935	𝓔	1951	𝒱		
1919	Ⓞ	Edw. VIII 1936	𝓕	Eliz. II 1952	𝒲		
1920	Ⓟ	Geo. VI 1937	𝒢	1953	𝒳		
1921	Ⓠ	1938	𝓗	1954	𝒴		
1922	Ⓡ			1955	𝒵		
1923	Ⓢ						

EDINBURGH

1956	A	1975	A	1991	R
1957	B	1976	B	1992	S
1958	C			1993	T
1959	D	1977	C	1994	U
1960	E			1995	V
1961	F			1996	W
1962	G	1978	D	1997	X
1963	H	1979	E	1998	Y
1964	J	1980	F		
1965	K	1981	G		
1966	L	1982	H		
1967	M	1983	I		
1968	N	1984	K		
1969	O	1985	L		
1970	P	1986	M		
1971	Q	1987	N		
1972	R	1988	O		
1973 31st Dec. 1974	S	1989	P		
		1990	Q		

Sequence discontinued upon introduction of the new marks under the Hallmarking Act 1973

70

EXETER

*c.*1570	⟨X⟩ ⟨IONS⟩					
*c.*1571	⟨II⟩ ⟨n⟩					
*c.*1575	⟨X⟩ ⟨❀⟩					
*c.*1580	⟨X⟩					
*c.*1585	⟨X⟩					
to						
*c.*1630	various					
*c.*1635	⟨X⟩					
to						
*c.*1675	⟨X⟩					
	variations of both					
*c.*1680	⟨X⟩					
*c.*1690	⟨X⟩					
	⟨X⟩ ⟨lion⟩					
*c.*1698	⟨X⟩ ⟨❀⟩					

	⟨castle⟩	⟨figure⟩	⟨lion⟩
1701		Ⓐ	
Anne 1702		Ⓑ	
1703		Ⓒ	
1704		Ⓓ	
1705		Ⓔ	
1706		Ⓕ	
1707		Ⓖ	
1708		Ⓗ	
1709		Ⓘ	
1710		Ⓚ	
1711		Ⓛ	
1712		Ⓜ	
1713		Ⓝ	
Geo. I 1714		Ⓞ	
1715		Ⓟ	
1716		Ⓠ	
1717		Ⓡ	
1718		Ⓢ	
1719		Ⓣ	
1720		Ⓥ	
	⟨castle⟩	⟨figure⟩	⟨lion⟩
1721		Ⓦ	
1722		Ⓧ	
1723		Ⓨ	
1724		Ⓩ	

71

EXETER

1725	a	1749	A	1773	A	
1726	b	1750	B	1774	B	
Geo. II. 1727	c	1751	C	1775	C	
1728	d	1752	D	1776	D	
1729	e	1753	E	1777	E	
1730	f	1754	F	1778	F	
1731	g	1755	G	1779	G	
1732	h	1756	H	1780	H	
1733	i	1757	I	1781-2	I	
1734	k	1758	K	1783	K	
1735	l	1759	L	1784	L	🐚
1736	m	Geo. III. 1760	M	1785	M	,,
1737	n	1761	N	1786	N	👤
1738	o	1762	O	1787	O	,,
1739	p	1763	P	1788	P	,,
1740	q	1764	Q	1789	q	,,
1741	r	1765	R	1790	r	,,
1742	s	1766	S	1791	f	,,
1743	t	1767	T	1792	t	,,
1744	u	1768	U	1793	u	,,
1745	w	1769	W	1794	W	,,
1746	x	1770	X	1795	X	,,
1747	y	1771	Y	1796	Y	,,
1748	z	1772	Z	Leopard's head not used after 1777		

EXETER

1797	A	"	1817	a	"	Vict. 1837	A	
1798	B	"	1818	b	"	1838	B	
1799	C		1819	c	"	1839	C	"
1800	D	"	Geo. IV. 1820	d	"	1840	D	"
1801	E	"	1821	e	"			
1802	F	"	1822	f		1841	E	"
1803	G	"	1823	g	"	1842	F	"
1804	H	"	1824	h	"			
			1825	i	"	1843	G	"
1805	I		1826	k	"	1844	H	"
1806	K	"	1827	l	"	1845	J	"
1807	L	"	1828	m	"	1846	K	"
1808	M	"	1829	n	"	1847	L	"
1809	N	"	Wm. IV. 1830	o	"	1848	M	"
1810	O	"				1849	N	"
1811	P	"	1831	p	"	1850	O	"
1812	Q	"	1832	q	"	1851	P	"
1813	R	"				1852	Q	"
1814	S	"	1833	r	"	1853	R	"
1815	T	"	1834	s		1854	S	"
1816	U	"	1835	t	"	1855	T	"
			1836	u	"	1856	U	"

EXETER

🏛	🦁	👑	🏛	🦁	👑
1857	Ⓐ	,,	1877	Ⓐ	,,
1858	Ⓑ	,,	1878	Ⓑ	,,
1859	Ⓒ	,,	1879	Ⓒ	,,
1860	Ⓓ	,,	1880	Ⓓ	,,
1861	Ⓔ	,,	1881	Ⓔ	,,
1862	Ⓕ	,,	1882	Ⓕ	,,
1863	Ⓖ	,,			
1864	Ⓗ	,,			
1865	Ⓘ	,,			
1866	Ⓚ	,,			
1867	Ⓛ	,,			
1868	Ⓜ	,,			
1869	Ⓝ	,,			
1870	Ⓞ	,,			
1871	Ⓟ	,,			
1872	Ⓠ	,,			
1873	Ⓡ	,,			
1874	Ⓢ	,,			
1875	Ⓣ	,,			
1876	Ⓤ	,,			

GLASGOW

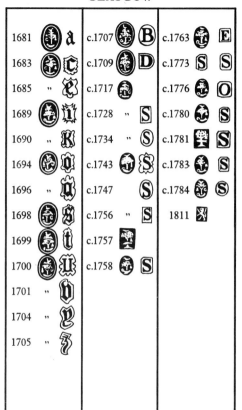

1681		c.1707	B	c.1763	E
1683		c.1709	D	c.1773	S
1685	"	c.1717		c.1776	O
1689		c.1728	" S	c.1780	S
1690	"	c.1734	" S	c.1781	S
1694		c.1743	S	c.1783	S
1696	"	c.1747	S	c.1784	S
1698		c.1756	" S	1811	
1699		c.1757			
1700		c.1758	S		
1701	"				
1704	"				
1705	"				

The maker's mark was stamped in duplicate on either side of the town mark up to the year 1784. From 1681-1705 a date letter was used. The letter "S" may have signified Standard. From 1784 to 1819 all Glasgow silver was marked in Edinburgh.

GLASGOW

1819	Ⓐ	,,	Vict. 1837	Ⓢ	,,	1853	𝕱	,,
Geo. IV 1820	Ⓑ	,,	1838	Ⓣ	,,	1854	𝕵	,,
1821	Ⓒ	,,	1839	Ⓤ	,,	1855	Ⓚ	,,
1822	Ⓓ	,,	1840	Ⓥ	,,	1856	Ⓛ	,,
1823	Ⓔ	,,	1841	Ⓦ	☺	1857	Ⓜ	,,
1824	Ⓕ	,,	1842	Ⓧ	,,	1858	Ⓝ	,,
1825	Ⓖ	,,	1843	Ⓨ	,,	1859	Ⓞ	,,
1826	Ⓗ	,,	1844	Ⓩ	,,	1860	Ⓟ	,,
1827	Ⓘ	,,				1861	Ⓠ	,,
1828	Ⓙ	,,	1845	Ⓐ	,,	1862	Ⓡ	,,
1829	Ⓚ	,,	1846	Ⓑ	,,	1863	Ⓢ	,,
Wm. IV 1830	Ⓛ	,,	1847	Ⓒ	,,	1864	Ⓣ	,,
1831	Ⓜ	,,	1848	Ⓓ	,,	1865	Ⓤ	,,
1832	Ⓝ	☺	1849	Ⓔ	,,	1866	Ⓥ	,,
1833	Ⓞ	,,	1850	Ⓕ	,,	1867	Ⓦ	,,
1834	Ⓟ	,,	1851	Ⓖ	,,	1868	Ⓧ	,,
1835	Ⓠ	,,	1852	Ⓗ	,,	1869	Ⓨ	,,
1836	Ⓡ	,,				1870	Ⓩ	,,

GLASGOW

🛡️ 🦁 👤			🛡️ 🦁 👑	
1871	Ⓐ	1897	Ⓐ
1872	Ⓑ	1898	Ⓑ
1873	Ⓒ	1899	Ⓒ
1874	Ⓓ	1900	Ⓓ
1875	Ⓔ	Edw. VII	
1876	Ⓕ	1901	Ⓔ
1877	Ⓖ	1902	Ⓕ
1878	Ⓗ	1903	Ⓖ
1879	Ⓘ	1904	Ⓗ
1880	Ⓙ	1905	Ⓘ
1881	Ⓚ	1906	Ⓙ
1882	Ⓛ	1907	Ⓚ
1883	Ⓜ	1908	Ⓛ
1884	Ⓝ	1909	Ⓜ
1885	Ⓞ	Geo. V	
1886	Ⓟ	1910	Ⓝ
1887	Ⓠ	1911	Ⓞ
1888	Ⓡ	1912	Ⓟ
1889	Ⓢ	1913	Ⓠ
1890	Ⓣ
1891	Ⓤ
1892	Ⓥ
1893	Ⓦ
1894	Ⓧ
1895	Ⓨ
1896	Ⓩ

🛡️ 🦁 👑	
1914	Ⓡ
1915	Ⓛ
1916	Ⓙ
1917	Ⓤ
1918	Ⓥ
1919	Ⓦ
1920	Ⓧ
1921	Ⓨ
1922	Ⓩ

🛡️ 🦁 👑	
1923	Ⓐ
1924	Ⓑ
1925	Ⓒ
1926	Ⓓ
1927	Ⓔ
1928	Ⓕ
1929	Ⓖ

GLASGOW

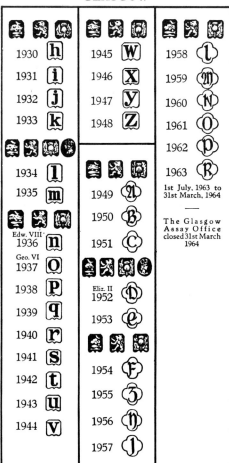

1930 **h**	1945 **W**	1958 **l**
1931 **i**	1946 **X**	1959 **m**
1932 **j**	1947 **y**	1960 **n**
1933 **k**	1948 **Z**	1961 **o**
1934 **l**	1949 **A**	1962 **p**
1935 **m**	1950 **B**	1963 **R**
Edw. VIII 1936 **n**	1951 **C**	1st July, 1963 to 31st March, 1964
Geo. VI 1937 **o**	Eliz. II 1952 **D**	The Glasgow Assay Office closed 31st March 1964
1938 **p**	1953 **e**	
1939 **q**	1954 **F**	
1940 **r**	1955 **J**	
1941 **s**	1956 **H**	
1942 **t**	1957 **I**	
1943 **u**		
1944 **v**		

NEWCASTLE

	Anne	1721 a
c. 1658 to c. 1670	1702 A	1722 B
	1703 B	1723 C
	1704 C	1724 D
	1705 D	1725 E
	1706 E	1726 F
	1707 F	Geo. II. 1727 G
c. 1672 to c. 1684	1708 G	
	1709	1728 H
c. 1685 to c. 1694	1710	1729 I
	1711	1730 K
c. 1696	1712 M	1731 L
	1713	1732 M
	Geo. I.	1733 N
	1714 N	1734 O
	1715	1735 P
	1716	1736 Q
c. 1700	1717 P	1737 R
	1718 Q	1738 S
	1719 R	1739 T
	1720 S	Between 1721 and 1728, shapes of shields and lion passant vary, and lion sometimes faces left.

79

NEWCASTLE

1740	A	1759	𝒜	1791	A	,,
1741	B	Geo. III. 1760-8	ℬ	1792	B	,,
1742	C	1769	𝒞	1793	C	,,
1743	D	1770	𝒟	1794	D	,,
1744	E	1771	ℰ	1795	E	,,
1745	F	1772	ℱ	1796	F	,,
1746	G	1773	G	1797	G	,,
1747	H	1774	H	1798	H	,,
1748	I	1775	I	1799	I	,,
1749	K	1776	K			
1750	L	1777	L	1800	K	,,
1751	M	1778	M	1801	L	,,
1752	N	1779	N	1802	M	,,
1753	O	1780	O	1803	N	
1754	P	1781	P	1804	O	,,
1755	Q	1782	Q	1805	P	,,
1756	R	1783	R	1806	Q	,,
1757	S	1784	S	1807	R	,,
1758	,,	1785	T	,,	1808	S	,,
		1786	U	1809	T	,,
		1787	W	,,	1810	U	,,
		1788	X	,,	1811	W	,,
		1789	Y	,,	1812	X	,,
		1790	Z	,,	1813	Y	,,
				1814	Z	,,

80

NEWCASTLE

1815 **A** ,,	1839 **A** ,,	1864 **ⓐ** ,,
1816 **B** ,,	1840 **B** ,,	1865 **ⓑ** ,,
1817 **C** ,,	1841 **C** ☺	1866 **ⓒ**
1818 **D** ,,	1842 **D** ,,	1867 **ⓓ** ,,
1819 **E** ,,	1843 **E** ,,	1868 **ⓔ** ,,
Geo. IV 1820 **F** ,,	1844 **F** ,,	1869 **ⓕ** ,,
1821 **G** ☺	1845 **G** ,,	1870 **ⓖ** ,,
1822 **H** ,,		1871 **ⓗ** ,,
1823 **I** ,,	1846 **H** ,,	1872 **ⓘ** ,,
1824 **K** ,,	1847 **I** ,,	1873 **ⓚ** ,,
1825 **L** ,,	1848 **J** ,,	1874 **ⓛ** ,,
1826 **M** ,,	1849 **K** ,,	1875 **ⓜ** ,,
1827 **N** ,,	1850 **L** ,,	1876 **ⓝ** ,,
1828 **O** ,,	1851 **M** ,,	1877 **ⓞ** ,,
1829 **P** ,,	1852 **N** ,,	1878 **ⓟ** ,,
Wm. IV 1830 **Q** ,,	1853 **O** ,,	1879 **ⓠ** ,,
1831 **R** ,,	1854 **P** ,,	1880 **ⓡ** ,,
1832 **S** ☺	1855 **Q** ,,	1881 **ⓢ** ,,
1833 **T** ,,	1856 **R** ,,	1882 **ⓣ** ,,
1834 **U** ,,	1857 **S** ,,	1883 **ⓤ** ,,
1835 **W** ,,	1858 **T** ,,	
1836 **X** ,,	1859 **U** ,,	
Vict. 1837 **Y** ,,	1860 **W** ,,	
1838 **Z** ,,	1861 **X** ,,	
	1862 **Y** ,,	
	1863 **Z** ,,	

81

NORWICH

Year	Mark	Letter		Year	Mark	Letter
1565		A				and variations thereof
1566		B		1624		Ⓐ
1567		C		1625		Ⓑ
1568		D		1626	Ⓒ	
1569		E		1627		Ⓓ
1570		F		1628	Ⓔ	
1571	"	G		1629		Ⓕ
1573	"	I		1630	Ⓖ	
1574	"	K		1631		Ⓗ
1579		P		1632	Ⓘ	
c. 1590				1633		Ⓚ
c. 1595				1634	Ⓛ	
c. 1600				1635		Ⓜ
c. 1610				1636	Ⓝ	
c. 1620				1637		Ⓞ
				1638	Ⓟ	
				1639		Ⓠ
				1640	Ⓡ	
				1641		Ⓢ
				1642	Ⓣ	
				1643		Ⓥ

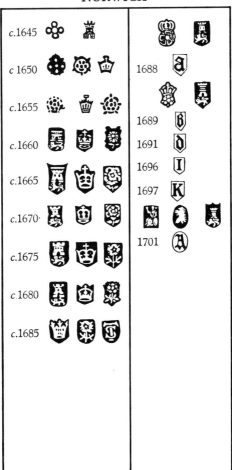

c.1645		
c 1650		
c.1655		
c.1660		
c.1665		
c.1670		
c.1675		
c.1680		
c.1685		

1688	
1689	
1691	
1696	
1697	
1701	

SHEFFIELD

Year	Date Letter		Year	Date Letter
1773	E		1798	V
1774	F		1799	E
1775	G		1800	N
1776	R		1801	H
1777	h		1802	M
1778			1803	F
1779	A		1804	G
1780	C		1805	B
1781	D		1806	A
1782	G		1807	S
1783	B		1808	P
1784	J		1809	K
1785	V		1810	L
1786	K		1811	C
1787	U		1812	D
1788			1813	R
1789			1814	W
1790	L		1815	O
1791	P		1816	T
1792	U		1817	X
1793	O		1818	I
1794	m		1819 Geo. IV	V
1795	q		1820	Q
1796	Z		1821	Y
1797	X		1822	Z

Mark shown in col. 6 was used on small objects to replace those in 3 and 4

From 15th July, 1797, for nine months, the Kings Head was duplicated owing to the Duty being doubled.

SHEFFIELD

Year						Year			
1823	🦀	👑	U	◉	ü		🦀	👑	☺
1824	🦀	👑	a	◉	ã	1848	E	E👑	"
1825	🦀	👑	b	◉	ḃ	1849	F	F👑	"
1826	🦀	👑	C	◉	ċ	1850	G	G👑	"
1827	🦀	👑	d	◉	ḋ	1851	H	H👑	"
1828	🦀	👑	e	◉	ė	1852	I	I👑	"
1829 Wm. IV	🦀	👑	f	◉	👑f	1853	K	K👑	"
1830	🦀	👑	g	◉	👑g	1854	L	☺	
1831	🦀	👑	h	◉	👑h	1855	M		"
1832	🦀	👑	k	◉	👑k	1856	N		"
1833	🦀	👑	l	◉	👑l	1857	O		"
1834	🦀	👑	m	◉	E👑	1858	P		"
1835	🦀	👑	P	◉	👑P	1859	R		"
1836 Vict.	🦀	👑	q	◉	👑q	1860	S		"
1837	🦀	👑	r	◉	r👑	1861	T		"
1838	🦀	👑	S	◉	S👑	1862	U		"
1839	🦀	👑	t	◉	t👑	1863	V		"
1840	🦀	👑	u	◉	u👑	1864	W		"
1841	🦀	👑	V	◉	V👑	1865	X		"
1842	🦀	👑	X	◉	X👑	1866	Y		"
1843	🦀	👑	Z	◉	Z👑	1867	Z		"
1844	🦀	👑	A	◉	A👑		🦀	👑	🌐
1845	🦀	👑	B	◉	B👑	1868	A		"
1846	🦀	👑	C	◉	C👑	1869	B		"
1847	🦀	👑	D	◉	D👑	1870	C		"
						1871	D		"
						1872	E		"

Mark shown in column 6 was used on small objects to replace those in 3 and 4.

SHEFFIELD

Year	Mark		Year	Mark	Year	Mark
1873	F	"	1893	a	1913	v
1874	G	"	1894	b	1914	w
1875	H	"	1895	c	1915	x
1876	J	"	1896	d	1916	y
1877	K	"	1897	e	1917	z
1878	L	"	1898	f		
1879	M	"	1899	g	1918	a
1880	N	"	1900	h	1919	b
1881	O	"	Edw. VII 1901	i	1920	c
1882	P	"	1902	k	1921	d
1883	Q	"	1903	l	1922	e
1884	R	"	1904	m	1923	f
1885	S	"	1905	n	1924	g
1886	T	"	1906	o	1925	h
1887	U	"	1907	p	1926	i
1888	V	"	1908	q	1927	k
1889	W	"	1909	r	1928	l
1890	X	"	Geo. V 1910	s	1929	m
1891	Y	"	1911	t	1930	n
1892	Z		1912	u	1931	o

86

SHEFFIELD

Year	Mark	Year	Mark	Year	Mark
1932	p	1945	C	1961	T
1933	q	1946	D	1962	U
1934	r	1947	E	1963	V
1935	s	1948	F	1964	W
Edw. VIII 1936	t	1949	G	1965	X
Geo. VI 1937	u	1950	H	1966	Y
1938	V	1951	I	1967	Z
1939	W	Eliz. II 1952	K	1968	A
1940	X	1953	L	1969	B
1941	y	1954	M	1970	C
1942	Z	1955	N	1971	D
1943	A	1956	O	1972	E
1944	B	1957	P	1973	F
		1958	Q		
		1959	R		
		1960	S		

Date letter of 1773 used for 1973 to commemorate bi-centenary of Sheffield Office.

1974 G

Sequence discontinued upon introduction of new marks under Hallmarking Act 1973.

SHEFFIELD

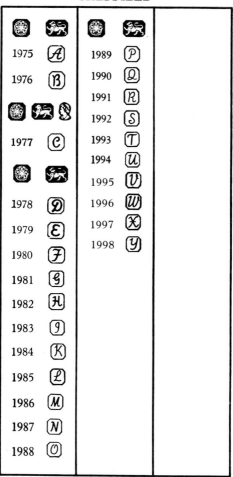

1975	A	1989	P
1976	B	1990	Q
		1991	R
1977	C	1992	S
		1993	T
1978	D	1994	U
1979	E	1995	V
1980	F	1996	W
1981	G	1997	X
1982	H	1998	Y
1983	I		
1984	K		
1985	L		
1986	M		
1987	N		
1988	O		

YORK

From about 1560 to 1606 variations of	From about 1560 to 1606 variations of	1607 to 1630 varies between
(1568)	(1583)	(1608) (1624)
(1577)	(1594)	1607 — a
		1608 — B
		1609 — C
Eliz.		1610 — D
1564 — F	1583 — a	1611 — E
1565 — G	1584 — b	1612 — F
1566 — H	1587 — c	1613 — G
1568 — K	1590 — h	1614 — H
1569 — L	1592 — k	1615 — J
1570 — M	1593 — l	1616 — k
1572 — O	1594 — m	1617 — L
1573 — P	1595 — n	1618 — M
1574 — Q	1596 — o	1619 — N
1575 — R	1597 — p	1620 — O
1576 — S	1598 — q	1621 — P
1577 — T	1599 — r	1622 — Q
1582 — Z	1601 — t	1623 — R
	Jas. I.	1624 — S
	1604 — r	Chas. I. 1625 — T
		1626 — U
		1627 — W
		1628 — X
		1629 — Y
		1630 — Z

89

1631 to 1656	1657 to 1681	1682 to 1699
1631 a	1657 A	(1680) (1696)
1632 b	1658 B	1682 A
1633 c	1659 C	1683 B
1634 d	Chas. II. 1660 D	1684 C
1635 e	1661 E	Jas. II. 1685 D
1636 f	1662 F	1686 E
1637 g	1663 G	1687 F
1638 h	1664 H	1688 G
1639 i	1665 J	Wm. & My. 1689 H
1641 k	1666 K	1690 J
1642 l	1667 L	1691 K
1643 m	1668 M	1692 L
1645 o	1669 N	1693 M
Comwth 1649 ſ	1670 O	1694 N
1650 t	1671 P	1695 O
1651 u	1672 Q	Wm. III. 1696 P
1652 v	1673 R	1697 Q
1653 w	1674 S	1698 R
1654 x	1675 T	1699 S
1655 y	1677 V	
1656 Z	1678 W	
	1679 X	
	1680 Y	
	1681 Z	

YORK

1700	𝒜	1787	A "	1812	a "
1701	B	1788	B "	1813	b "
Anne 1702	C	1789	C or C "	1814	c "
1703	D	1790	d "	1815	d "
1705	F	1791	e "	1816	e "
1706	G	1792	f "	1817	f "
1708	ⓐ	1793	g "	1818	g "
1711	ⓜ	1794	h "	1819 Geo. IV 1820	i "
1713	ⓦ	1795	i "	1821	k "
No plate yet found bearing date letter between 1713 to 1778		1796	k ⓑ	1822	l "
		1797	L "	1823	m "
		1798	M "	1824	n "
Geo. III. 1778	C	1799	N "	1825	o "
1779	D	1800	O "	1826	p "
1780	E	1801	P " :	1827	q "
1781	F	1802	Q "	1828	r "
1782	G	1803	R "	1829 Wm. IV 1830	s "
1783	H	1804	S "	1831	t ⓒ
1784	J ⓓ	1805	T "	1832	u "
1785	K "	1806	U "	1833	v "
1786	L ⓔ	1807	V "	1834	w "
		1808	W "	1835	x "
		1809	X "	1836	y "
		1810	Y "		z "
		1811	Z "		

Lion found for 1803 and 1806 facing right

YORK

Vict.		
1837 **A** ,,		
1838 **B** ,,		
1839 **C** ,,		
1840 **D** 🜚		
1841 **E** ,,		
1842 **F** ,,		
1843 **G** ,,		
1844 **H** ,,		
1845 **I** ,,		
1846 **K** ,,		
1847 **L** ,,		
1848 **M** ,,		
1849 **N** ,,		
1850 **O** ,,		
1851 **P** ,,		
1852 **Q** ,,		
1853 **R** ,,		
1854 **S** ,,		
1855 **T** ,,		
1856 **V** ,,		

Leopard's head
not used after
1850

For evidence as to certain alterations and additional date letters, see
"York Assay Office & Silversmiths 1776-1858" by Martin Gubbins
(Pub: Wm. Sessions Ltd., York. 1983).

92

MARKS USED BY MINOR GUILDS

ENGLAND

	about	about	
Barnstaple .	1370 to	1730	
Bristol ...	1730 ,,	1800	
Hull......	1570 ,,	1710	
King's Lynn	1600 ,,	1700	
Leeds.....	1650 ,,	1700	
Lincoln ...	1420 ,,	1710	
Plymouth ..	1600 ,,	1700	
Taunton ...	1640 ,,	1700	

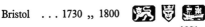

SCOTLAND

	about	about	
Aberdeen ..	1650 ,,	1880	
Arbroath...	1830 ,,	1840	
Banff.....	1680 ,,	1850	
Canongate..	1560 ,,	1784	
Dumfries ..	1790 ,,	1840	
Dundee ...	1570 ,,	1845	

MARKS USED BY MINOR GUILDS

SCOTLAND—continued

Elgin . . . . . about 1700 to about 1840   **ELGIN** or 🧍 or 🏰

Greenock . . 1760 ,, 1840   ⚓ or 🚢 or Ⓖ or 👤

Inverness . . 1685 ,, 1880   **INS** or 🅹 or 🐄

Montrose . . 1680 ,, 1830   🌸 or 🌸 or 🌸

Perth . . . . . 1612 ,, 1860   🦅 or 🦅

Tain . . . . . . 1720 ,, 1830   **TAIN**

Wick . . . . . 1840 ,, 1860   **WICK**

IRELAND

Cork . . . . . about 1660 to about 1840   🏰 🚢 🏰 🍶 or **STERLING**

Galway . . . . 1640 ,, 1750   ⚓ or ⚓ or 🌸

Kilkenny . . . 1650 ,, 1700   🏰

Limerick . . . 1700 ,, 1800   or

Youghal . . . 1650 ,, 1720   ⚓ or 🛡️

CHANNEL ISLANDS
Guernsey.. 1690 „ 1750

Jersey..... 1760 „ 1830

SOUTH AFRICA
Cape of Good Hope, 1715 to 1790

Old Sheffield Plate

For full particulars of the craft and general information, see *History of Old Sheffield Plate,* by Frederick Bradbury (originally published by Macmillan & Co., Ltd., 1912 and published again, in the original edition, by J. W. Northend Ltd., Sheffield, 1968); also *Old Silver Platers and their Marks,* by B. W. Watson, M.A., Sheffield Assay Office.

SHEFFIELD PLATE

is the term used to denote articles made of copper coated with silver by fusion, invented in 1742 by Thomas Boulsover. This process lapsed on the introduction of the method of silver-plating by electro-deposition about the middle of the 19th century.

MARKS

These can be divided into three groups and will be of great assistance to collectors as a means of identifying both the period and maker of a specimen bearing marks. Though of great use as a general guide, these marks cannot be relied upon for absolute accuracy of date owing to the absence of any date letters associated with the maker's marks.

GROUP I.

The earliest record of a mark probably synchronizes with the first production of Joseph Hancock circa 1755 **IH** his initial punch closely resembled the contemporary London silversmiths' punches. A few years later we find **IZ** Law's initials associated with his full name **TH°LAW** Then H. Tudor's device 1760 **HT** repeated three times, more closely resembling the marks on solid silver articles than former representations. This marking of earlier made Sheffield Plate terminated in 1772, owing to successful agitation by London silversmiths.

GROUP II.

By the year 1784, the Sheffield Plate manu-facturers were successful in obtaining an Act which authorized their marking of goods with a device associated with the maker's name

These regulations, however were not very strictly adhered to and we find many examples where the registered mark appears unassociated with name of maker; this, in fact, became the more frequent form of marking early in the 19th century.

GROUP III.

About the year 1805, there suddenly sprang into use a large quantity of spoons, forks, dessert knives, fish servers, skewers, and many other articles described as "flat ware" for domestic use. The surface was plated with thin sheets of silver attached thereto by solder; this process was described as "close plating." As the origin of this method was associated with the town of Birmingham, it will be found that a great influx of makers' marks was registered in Sheffield by the producers of Close Plate in that town in the year 1807.

By the Act of 1784, any maker of goods plated with silver or made to look like silver, within 100 miles of Sheffield, who desired to place a mark thereon had to register the same at the Sheffield Silver Assay Office, and Birmingham makers consequently came within the scope of this Act.

The last registration of marks recorded for either Sheffield Plate or Close Plated articles at the Sheffield Office was in the year 1836.

The Crown as a mark was used frequently between the years 1765 and 1825 by various makers as a guarantee of quality.

98

OLD SHEFFIELD PLATE

OLD SHEFFIELD PLATE MARKS
and those struck on Silver-plated Steel Cutlery described as "Close Plate".

Date	Name of Firm	Makers' Marks
1743	Boulsover Thomas ...	No Mark Traced.
1755	Hancock Joseph ...	IOSᴴ HANCOCK SHEFFIELD. **IH**
1756	Smith Nathaniel ...	**NS**
1758	Law Thomas ...	𝑇𝐿 THᵒ LAW 𝑇𝐿 𝑇𝐿 **LAW** 𝑇𝐿
1760	Tudor & Leader ...	𝒦 𝒯&𝑒ᵒ 𝐓𝐋 𝐓𝐋 𝐓𝐋 𝐓𝐋 𝐓𝐋 𝐓𝐋
1760	Fenton Matthew & Co.	𝕾 𝕾 𝕾 𝕾
1760	Unidentified	𝔇 𝔇 𝔇
1760	Unidentified	🙶 🙶 🙶
1760	Unidentified	𝐢𝐝 𝐢𝐝 𝐢𝐝 𝐢𝐝
1764	Hoyland John & Co.	𝕵𝕮 𝕵𝕮 𝕵𝕮 𝕵𝕮 𝕵 𝕮 𝕮 𝕮
1764	Boulton & Fothergill	☺ **B·F** ☺
1765	Roberts Jacob & Samuel	**JSR**

1765	Winter John & Co. ...	
1765	Morton Richard ...	
1768	Rowbotham J. & Co.	
1770	Ashforth, Ellis & Co.	
1770	Ryland William ...	No Mark Traced.
1772	Littlewood J. ...	PLATED

No marks legalized between 1773 and 1784		
1784	Ashforth G. & Co. ...	
1784	Fox T. & Co. ...	
1784	Green W. & Co. ...	
1784	Holy D., Wilkinson & Co	
1784	Law T. & Co. ...	
1784	Parsons J. & Co. ...	
1784	Smith N. & Co. ...	
1784	Staniforth, Parkin & Co.	
1784	Sykes & Co.	
1784	Tudor, Leader & Nicholson	

1784	Boulton M. & Co. ...	
1784	Dixon T. & Co. ...	
1784	Holland H. & Co. ...	
1784	Moore J.	
1784	Smith & Co.	
1785	Beldon, Hoyland & Co.	
1785	Brittain, Wilkinson & Brownill	
1785	Deakin, Smith & Co. ...	
1785	Love J. & Co. ... ... (Love, Silverside, Darby & Co.)	
1785	Morton R. & Co. ...	
1785	Roberts, Cadman & Co.	
1786	Roberts J. & S. ...	
1786	Sutcliffe R. & Co. ...	
1787	Bingley W.	
1788	Madin F. & Co. ...	
1789	Jervis W.	

1790	Colmore S.	
1794	Goodwin E.	
1795	Watson, Fenton & Bradbury	
1797	Froggatt, Coldwell & Lean	
1799	Green J. & Co. ...	
1800	Goodman, Gainsford & Fairbairn	
1803	Ellerby W.	
1803	Garnett W.	
1804	Holy D., Parker & Co.	
1804	Newbould W. & Son ...	
1805	Drabble I. & Co. ...	
1806	Coldwell W.	
1806	Hill D. & Co.	
1807	Law J. & Son	
1807	Butts T.	
1807	Green J.	

1807	Hutton W.	
1807	Law R.	
1807	Linwood J.	
1807	Linwood W.	
1807	Meredith H.	
1807	Peake	
1807	Ryland W. & Son ...	
1807	Scot W.	
1807	Silkirk W.	
1807	Thomason E. & Dowler	
1807	Tonks Samuel	
1807	Waterhouse & Co. ...	
1807	Wilmore Joseph ...	
1808	Gainsford R.	
1808	Hatfield A.	
1808	Banister W.	

1808	Gibbs G.	
1808	Hipkiss J.	
1808	Horton D.	
1808	Lea A. C.	
1808	Linwood M. & Sons ...	
1808	Nicholds J.	
1809	Beldon G.	
1809	Wright J. & Fairbairn G.	
1809	Cheston T.	
1809	Harrison J.	
1809	Hipwood W.	
1809	Horton J.	
1809	Silk R.	
1809	Howard S. & T. ...	
1810	Smith, Tate, Nicholson & Hoult	
1810	Dunn G. B.	
1810	Hanson M.	
1810	Pimley S.	

1811	Creswick T. & J. ...	CRESWICKS
1811	Stot B.	Stot
1811	Watson, Pass & Co. (late J. Watson)	WATSON PASS&Cº
1811	Lees G.	LEES
1811	Pearson R.	PEAR SON
1811	White J. (White & Allgood)	WHITE
1812	Kirkby S.	KIRKBY FOR USE
1812	Allgood J.	ALL GOOD
1812	Allport E.	All port All port
1812	Gilbert J.	Gil bert Gil bert
1812	Hinks J.	HINKS
1812	Johnson J.	JOHN SON
1812	Small T.	SMALL
1812	Smith W.	SM ITH
1813	Younge S. & C. & Co....	S.C.YOUNGE &Cº
1813	Thomas S.	THO MAS
1813	Tyndall J.	TYN DALL
1814	Best H.	BEST
1814	Cracknall J.	CRACK NALL

OLD SHEFFIELD PLATE

1814	Jordan T.	
1814	Woodward W. ...	
1815	Lilly John	
1816	Best & Wastidge ...	
1816	Ashley	
1816	Davis J.	
1816	Evans S.	
1816	Freeth H.	
1816	Harwood T.	
1816	Lilly Joseph	
1816	Turley S.	
1817	Cope C. G.	
1817	Pemberton & Mitchell	
1817	Shephard J.	
1818	Markland W.	
1819	Corn J. & J. Sheppard...	
1819	Rogers J.	

1820	Hall W.	
1820	Moore F.	
1820	Turton J.	
1821	Blagden, Hodgson & Co.	
1821	Holy D. & G. ...	
1821	Needham C.	
1821	Sansom T. & Sons ...	
1821	Child T.	
1821	Smith I.	
1821	Worton S.	
1822	Rodgers J. & Sons ...	
1822	Bradshaw J.	
1823	Briggs W.	
1823	Harrison G.	
1823	Smallwood J.	
1824	Causer J. F.	

1824	Jones	
1824	Tonks & Co.	
1828	Roberts, Smith & Co. ...	
1828	Smith J. & Son ...	
1828	Askew	A SKEW MAKER NOTTINGHAM
1829	Hall Henry	
1829	Hobday J.	
1830	Watson J. & Son ...	
1830	Bishop Thomas ...	
1831	Hutton W.	
1833	Atkin Henry	
1833	Waterhouse I. & I. & Co.	
1833	Watson W.	W WATSON MAKER SHEFFIELD
1835	Dixon J. & Sons ...	

1836	Smith J.	JOSEPHUS SMITH
1836	Waterhouse, Hatfield & Co.	
1836	Wilkinson H. & Co. ...	
1837	Hutton W.	Hutton ☺ Hutton ☺
1839	Hutton W.	H & S T
1839	Prime J.	
1840	Walker, Knowles & Co.	
1842	Waterhouse George & Co.	W & C S
1848	Smith, Sissons & Co. ...	
1849	Padley, Parkin & Co. ...	
1849	Hutton W.	W H & S T
1850	Mappin Bros.	MAP PIN BROT HERS
1860	Oldham T.	
1860	Robert & Briggs ...	R & B X

From 1840 to 1860 nickel silver gradually superseded the use of copper, and articles were produced by the aid of both processes; though the bodies of larger pieces continued to be constructed of fused plated metal, the other parts were subjected to the process of electro deposition.

The following marks have been used extensively on nickel silver articles plated by the process of electro-deposition.

The Bell   The Hand   The Cross Arrows

The Pineapple   The Cross Keys

—◆—

Devices on Plated articles, as illustrated above, were in vogue after the cessation of registrations of Sheffield Plate Marks at the Sheffield Office. As they too closely resembled the Sheffield Silver Assay Marks, the use of the Crown was prohibited in 1896.

NOTES

NOTES